The Complete Books of Enoch

Ancient Apocalyptic Writings That Reveal the Secrets of Heaven, the Origins of Demons, and the End Times

A Modern Translation

Adapted for the Contemporary Reader

Various Ancient Writers

Translated by Tim Zengerink

Table of Contents

Preface - Message to the Reader

What If You Could Help Rebuild the Greatest Library in Human History?

Thousands of years ago, the Library of Alexandria stood as the crown jewel of human achievement — a sanctuary where the collected wisdom of every known civilization was gathered, preserved, and shared freely.

And then, it was lost.

Through fire, conquest, and the slow erosion of time, humanity lost not just books — but ideas, dreams, discoveries, and stories that could have changed the world forever.

Today, the Library of Alexandria lives again — and you are invited to be a part of its restoration.

Our mission is simple yet profound:

To rebuild the greatest library the world has ever known, and to translate all timeless works into every language and dialect, so that no seeker of knowledge is ever left behind again.

By joining our movement to rebuild the modern Library of Alexandria, you become part of an unprecedented mission:

- **Unlimited Access to the Greatest Audiobooks & eBooks Ever Written:**

  Instantly explore thousands of legendary works—Plato, Shakespeare, Jane Austen, Leo Tolstoy, and countless more. All instantly available to read or listen, placing a complete literary universe at your fingertips.

- **Beautiful Paperback & Deluxe Editions at Printing Cost**

  Own any title as an elegant paperback, deluxe hardcover, or stunning collectible boxset—offered to you at true printing cost, delivered straight to your door. Build your personal Library of Alexandria, crafted for beauty, built for durability, and worthy of proud display.

- **Fresh Translations for Modern Readers—in Every Language & Dialect**

  Enjoy timeless masterpieces reimagined in clear, contemporary language—no more outdated phrases or obscure references. Alongside the original versions, we're tirelessly translating these classics into every language and dialect imaginable, ensuring accessibility and understanding across cultures and generations.

- **Join a Global Renaissance of Literature & Knowledge**

  You directly support expanding our library, publishing deluxe editions at true cost, translating works into all global languages, and bringing humanity's greatest stories to people everywhere. By joining today, you're not just preserving a legacy of masterpieces; you set in motion a powerful wave of literary accessibility.

Become a Torchbearer of Knowledge.

Join us for free now at **LibraryofAlexandria.com**

Together, we will ensure that the light of human wisdom never fades again.

With gratitude and a shared love of knowledge,
The Modern Library of Alexandria Team

Visit:

www.libraryofalexandria.com

Or scan the code below:

Introduction

The Lost Revelation of Enoch:
Origins, Judgment, and the Secrets of Heaven

Among the apocryphal and pseudepigraphal texts that orbit the canon of the Bible, no collection has held the fascination, mystique, and spiritual weight of the Books of Enoch. Once widely read by early Jewish and Christian communities, these writings were ultimately excluded from the mainstream biblical canon—deemed too speculative, mystical, or controversial to be accepted alongside the Torah or the Gospels. Yet their influence never disappeared. From the writings of the early Church Fathers to medieval mystics and modern scholars, the Enochian texts have continued to echo through the corridors of sacred thought, offering visions of angels and demons, heaven and hell, cosmic rebellion and divine justice.

The figure of Enoch first appears briefly in the Book of Genesis: "Enoch walked with God; then he was no more, because God took him" (Genesis 5:24). This mysterious line suggests an ascension—a divine favor that allowed Enoch to bypass death and enter directly into the heavenly realm. What did he see there? What was he taught? What messages did he return with? The Books of Enoch answer these questions with vivid detail, constructing one of the most elaborate apocalyptic cosmologies of any ancient text.

This edition brings together the three major Books of Enoch—Enoch I (The Book of Enoch), Enoch II (The Book of the Secrets of Enoch), and Enoch III (The Hebrew Book of Enoch)—as well as the fragmented but essential Book of Giants. Together, they offer a panoramic view of Enoch's revelations and provide a narrative arc that spans the fall of the Watchers, the birth of the Nephilim, divine judgment, visions of paradise, celestial hierarchies, and apocalyptic

4

prophecy. Each book contributes a unique voice, theological emphasis, and esoteric insight, but they are united in portraying Enoch not only as a prophet, but as a cosmic scribe, an intermediary between heaven and earth, and a seer of divine mysteries.

Enoch I: The Book of Enoch

Also known as 1 Enoch or the Ethiopic Book of Enoch, this is the most well-known and widely studied of the Enochian writings. It consists of several sections, including the Book of the Watchers, The Similitudes (Parables) of Enoch, The Astronomical Book, The Book of Dream Visions, and The Epistle of Enoch. Written between the third century BCE and the first century CE, the text presents Enoch as the recipient of divine revelations delivered by angels.

At the core of Enoch I is the dramatic story of the Watchers— angels who descended to Earth, lusted after human women, and gave birth to the Nephilim, giant hybrid beings whose violence and appetite corrupted the Earth. This narrative not only expands on the cryptic lines of Genesis 6:1–4, but also introduces one of the earliest Jewish demonologies. The Watchers are punished, the Nephilim destroyed, and Enoch is taken on a heavenly journey where he sees the structure of the cosmos, the places of the dead, and the fate of the righteous and the wicked.

In the Similitudes, Enoch receives Messianic prophecies and visions of the final judgment, including the role of the "Son of Man," a title that will resonate in later Christian theology. The Astronomical Book details the movement of celestial bodies, linking astronomy to divine law. The Dream Visions recount Israel's history and predict its future. In every section, the Book of Enoch blends narrative drama with theological insight, offering an apocalyptic worldview that would later influence the Book of Revelation, the Dead Sea Scrolls, and early Christian eschatology.

Enoch II: The Book of the Secrets of Enoch

Also called 2 Enoch or the Slavonic Enoch, this lesser-known but equally profound text was likely composed between the first century BCE and the first century CE. It survives primarily in Old Church Slavonic and reflects a mystical, liturgical tradition. In this book, Enoch is taken by angels through the ten heavens. Each level reveals a new dimension of creation—from the angelic realms to the throne of God.

Here, Enoch is not just a witness but a transformed being. He is clothed in divine garments, anointed with light, and granted access to the secrets of creation, time, and the soul. The cosmology of 2 Enoch is deeply symbolic and introduces themes of repentance, righteousness, and divine measurement. It explores the idea that every deed is recorded, every soul tested, and every heart weighed on divine scales. The text concludes with Enoch's return to Earth, his final instructions to his sons, and his eventual assumption into heaven.

What distinguishes Enoch II is its intensely personal tone. Enoch speaks not only as a prophet but as a father and teacher. His message is moral, mystical, and filled with urgency. The book bridges the visionary tradition of apocalyptic literature with the moral demands of wisdom literature, offering guidance not just about the end of the world, but about how to live righteously within it.

Enoch III: The Hebrew Book of Enoch

Enoch III, or the Sefer Hekhalot, emerges from the Jewish mystical tradition known as Merkavah or Hekhalot mysticism. Likely composed between the third and sixth centuries CE, this text recounts Enoch's transformation into the angel Metatron—a being of immense power who sits next to the divine throne.

Here, Enoch ascends not just to observe, but to participate in the workings of heaven. He learns the secret names of God, the configurations of the heavenly palaces, and the ranks of angelic orders. The text is densely symbolic and rooted in esoteric practices of prayer, incantation, and divine ascent.

While it may differ in tone and structure from the earlier books, Enoch III continues the central themes of divine knowledge, spiritual elevation, and the transformation of the human into the angelic. It reflects a theological evolution where the boundaries between human and divine are explored and transcended. The idea of Enoch becoming Metatron becomes a cornerstone of later Kabbalistic speculation and reinforces the notion that the righteous can ascend to unimaginable spiritual heights.

The Book of Giants

Preserved in fragments, especially among the Dead Sea Scrolls, the Book of Giants expands the narrative of the Watchers and their monstrous offspring. It offers the perspective of the giants themselves—beings plagued by visions of judgment and desperate for salvation. They seek Enoch's intercession and receive divine decrees of destruction.

Though fragmented, this text is invaluable for understanding the psychological and theological dimensions of the Watchers' story. It presents the Nephilim not simply as villains, but as tragic figures—born of sin, doomed by prophecy, and caught in a cosmic drama beyond their control.

A Legacy Reclaimed

The Books of Enoch challenge the boundaries of canon, theology, and spiritual imagination. They pose hard questions about justice, divine mercy, cosmic order, and human destiny. Why do the innocent suffer? What happens after death? Is there hope for the fallen? Can humans participate in divine wisdom? These texts do not offer easy answers—but they do offer vision, depth, and awe.

Their exclusion from the Bible was not due to lack of relevance, but because of their power. They were too mystical, too strange, too uncontainable for the theological frameworks of later councils. Yet today, they return—not as heresy, but as heritage. Not as threats to orthodoxy, but as reminders of the spiritual hunger and apocalyptic hope that defined the faith of many ancient believers.

This modern translation presents the Enochian texts with clarity, reverence, and contextual insight. Archaic language has been refined, obscure symbols illuminated, and theological themes explored. The goal is to make these profound scriptures accessible without diminishing their mystery.

Whether you read these books as sacred truth, spiritual allegory, or historical literature, one thing is clear: they have the power to move, to provoke, and to awaken. Enoch walked with God—and in these pages, you are invited to walk with him.

May these revelations stir your soul, expand your vision, and lead you into deeper understanding of the heavens above, the battles below, and the divine wisdom that holds all things together.

Enoch I
The Book of Enoch
(Ethiopic Enoch)

The Books of Enoch, said to be written by the ancient figure Enoch, are important religious texts. Some early Jewish and Christian groups valued them because they describe powerful visions, secrets of the heavens, and messages from God. Even though these books are not included in the Hebrew Bible or most Christian Bibles, they still give insight into what people believed during the time of the Second Temple and early Christianity.

These writings talk about fallen angels, the structure of heaven, and what might happen to humanity in the future. They reveal how people of that era understood the world, using striking images and deep spiritual ideas.

Adding these texts to this collection makes the Apocrypha even richer, allowing readers to explore different ancient religious beliefs. They also raise important questions about God's justice, life's purpose, and how the universe is organized.

Chapter I

Enoch's words of blessing were given to those who are chosen and live rightly. He spoke to those who will be alive during a time of great trouble when all the wicked and godless will be removed.

Enoch, a righteous man, received a vision from God. His eyes were opened, and he saw the Holy One in the heavens. The angels showed him this vision, and he came to understand everything they revealed. But this message was not meant for his own time—it was for a future generation.

He spoke about those who were chosen and delivered this message:

The Great and Holy One will leave His dwelling place.
The eternal God will come down to the earth, even to Mount
    Sinai.
He will step out from His camp
And show His great power from the highest heavens.

People everywhere will be filled with fear,
And even the Watchers—mighty beings—will tremble.
Terror will spread across the whole world.
The strongest mountains will shake,
And high hills will be flattened.
They will melt like wax in a blazing fire.

The earth itself will crack apart,
And everything on it will be destroyed.
A great judgment will come upon all people.

But those who live rightly will have peace.
God will protect the ones He has chosen,
And His kindness will surround them.

They will belong to Him completely,
And they will thrive.
They will receive His blessing,
And He will care for each one of them.
His light will shine on them,
And He will fill them with peace.
And look—He will come with tens of thousands of His holy
    ones

To bring justice to all people,
To remove the wicked,
And to judge everyone for their ungodly actions
And the harsh words they have spoken against Him.

Chapter II

Look up at the sky and see how everything moves in order. The stars and other lights follow their paths, rising and setting at the right times. They never change the pattern set for them.

Now look at the earth and notice everything that happens from one end to the other. The land stays firm and steady, never changing. Everything on it continues as it has been, showing the work of God for all to see.

Think about the seasons—summer and winter. See how the earth is covered with water, and how the clouds, dew, and rain settle over the land.

Chapter III

During winter, most trees look dried up and lose all their leaves. But there are fourteen kinds of trees that don't do this. Instead of shedding their leaves, they hold onto them for two to three years until fresh ones grow.

Chapter IV

Watch how the sun sits high in the sky during summer, shining straight down on the land. The heat is so strong that you look for shade to cool off. Even the ground and rocks get so hot that walking on them becomes impossible.

Chapter V

Notice how trees grow fresh green leaves and bear fruit. Pay attention to the world around you and see that the One who lives forever has created everything this way. His works continue in the same cycle, year after year, just as He intended. Everything follows His plan, and nothing changes from what He has commanded.

Look at the seas and rivers too. They follow their course exactly as He directed, never straying from His orders.

But you have not remained faithful. You have not followed the Lord's commands. Instead, you have turned away and spoken with pride, using harsh words against Him. Because of your stubbornness and hardened hearts, you will not find peace.

As a result, you will regret your days, and your years will end in disaster. Your suffering will grow, leading to eternal punishment with no mercy.

During that time, your names will be used as a lasting curse by those who do what is right. People will use your name when they wish harm upon others, and sinners and those without faith will be condemned just as you are. For those who reject God, only a curse remains.

But those who are righteous will be filled with joy. Their sins will be forgiven, and they will receive mercy, peace, and patience. Salvation will come to them, bringing light and hope.

For sinners, there will be no salvation—only a curse. But for the chosen ones, there will be light, happiness, and peace. They will inherit the earth.

Wisdom will be given to them, and they will live without sin. They will not fall into arrogance or wrongdoing, and those who are wise will remain humble.

They will not turn away from what is right, nor will they sin again. They will not die as a result of judgment or anger. Instead, they will live full and peaceful lives, filled with joy. Their happiness will continue forever, and they will enjoy true peace for all their days.

Chapter VI

As people on Earth grew in number, they had daughters who were beautiful. The angels, who came from heaven, saw them and wanted to be with them. They said to each other, "Let's choose wives from among these women and have children with them."

Their leader, Semjâzâ, was unsure and said, "I'm afraid you won't all go through with this plan, and I'll be the only one punished for committing such a great sin." But the others reassured him, saying, "Let's all make a promise together and swear an oath. We will not abandon this plan but will see it through."

So they all swore an oath and made a binding agreement to carry it out. There were two hundred of them in total, and during the time of Jared, they came down to the top of Mount Hermon. They named it Mount Hermon because it was the place where they made their oath and sealed it with a curse.

These were their leaders: Semjâzâ, their chief, along with Arâkîba, Râmêêl, Kôkabîêl, Tâmîêl, Râmîêl, Dânêl, Êzêqêêl, Barâqîjâl, Asâêl, Armârôs, Batârêl, Anânêl, Zaqîêl, Samsâpêêl, Satarêl, Tûrêl, Jômjâêl, and Sariêl. Each of them led a group of ten.

Chapter VII

The others also took wives for themselves, each choosing one. They lived with them and corrupted themselves. They taught the women magical spells, charms, and how to use roots and different plants.

The women became pregnant and gave birth to gigantic children, growing to an unbelievable height. These giants ate everything that people had worked hard to produce. When there was no longer enough food, they turned on the humans and started to eat them instead.

The giants also committed terrible acts against birds, animals, reptiles, and fish. They even began to eat each other's flesh and drink blood. Because of their wickedness, the earth cried out against them.

Chapter VIII

Azâzêl taught people how to make weapons like swords, knives, shields, and armor. He showed them how to work with metals found in the earth. He also introduced jewelry-making, the use of antimony for makeup, and ways to make the eyes look more attractive. He revealed the secrets of precious stones and different colorful dyes.

Because of this, people became more wicked. They fell into immorality, were deceived, and grew more corrupt in their ways. Semjâzâ taught them spells and how to use plant roots for magic. Armârôs showed them how to break enchantments. Barâqîjâl taught astrology, while Kôkabêl revealed the mysteries of the stars. Ezêqêêl explained how to read cloud patterns, Araqiêl taught the signs of the earth, Shamsiêl revealed the secrets of the sun, and Sariêl explained how the moon moves.

As people suffered and died, their cries of pain reached up to heaven.

Chapter IX

Michael, Uriel, Raphael, and Gabriel looked down from heaven and saw that the earth was filled with violence and wrongdoing. They said to each other, "The earth, which was meant to be a peaceful place, is now crying out because of the suffering, and its cries have reached the gates of heaven.

The souls of people are begging us, the holy ones in heaven, to bring their case before the Most High."

Then they spoke to the Lord, saying, "Mighty God, King of kings, ruler over all things, Your throne has stood for all time, and Your name is holy, glorious, and blessed forever.

You created everything, and You have power over all things. Nothing is hidden from You—everything is clear before Your eyes.

You see what Azâzêl has done. He has taught people evil ways and revealed secrets that were meant to stay in heaven—things humans were never supposed to know.

And Semjâzâ, whom You put in charge of his followers, has come down to the earth and taken human women as his own. He and his companions have sinned with them and taught them sinful ways.

Now, their children, the giants, have brought destruction, and the earth is filled with violence and corruption because of them.

The souls of those who have died are crying out for justice, and their voices have reached heaven. Their sorrow will not stop because of all the wickedness happening on earth.

Lord, You knew all of this before it happened. You see what is going on, yet You have not told us what we should do about it."

Chapter X

Then the Most High, the Holy and Great One, spoke and sent Uriel to Lamech's son. He told him, "Go to Noah and warn him in My name. Tell him to hide himself and reveal to him what is about to happen. A great flood will soon cover the earth and destroy everything. Tell him how to survive so that he and his descendants can continue for all generations."

Then the Lord spoke to Raphael, saying, "Capture Azâzêl, tie him up, and throw him into the darkness. Dig a deep pit in the desert of Dûdâêl and cast him into it. Cover him with sharp, jagged rocks and block out all light so that he never sees it again. He will remain there forever. On the day of the final judgment, he will be thrown into the fire. Heal the earth from the corruption caused by the fallen angels so that the plague they brought may end. This way, humanity will not be destroyed because of the forbidden knowledge the Watchers have shared. The whole earth has been ruined by the things Azâzêl has taught, so place all the blame for sin on him."

Then the Lord said to Gabriel, "Go after the evil ones and those born from forbidden unions. Destroy the children of the fallen angels and make them fight each other until they wipe themselves out. They will not live long lives. If their fathers plead for them, do not listen, for they believe they will live forever and expect to reach five hundred years."

The Lord then spoke to Michael, saying, "Go and capture Semjâzâ and his followers, who have taken human women and made themselves unclean with them."

Once their sons have destroyed one another, and they have watched their loved ones perish, bind them for seventy generations deep within the earth. Keep them there until the final judgment, when they will be condemned forever. At that time, they will be cast into the fiery abyss, suffering in a prison where they will be locked away for eternity. Those who are sentenced to destruction will remain with them until the end of all generations.

Wipe out the spirits of the wicked and the children of the fallen angels, for they have harmed humanity. Remove all sin from the earth and put an end to evil. Let righteousness and truth take root and grow. It will bring blessings, and goodness will remain forever in joy and peace.

Then the righteous will be saved. They will live long lives, having thousands of children, and will enjoy both their youth and old age in peace.

After that, the whole earth will be restored to goodness. It will be covered with trees and filled with blessings. Every kind of tree will grow, and vineyards will be planted, producing an abundance of grapes. Crops will yield a thousand times more than before, and olive trees will produce ten times more oil.

Cleanse the world of all oppression, wickedness, and sin. Remove every trace of evil, wiping it completely from the earth.

All people will become righteous, and every nation will give Me honor and praise. They will worship Me together. The earth will be purified from all corruption, sin, and suffering, and I will never again bring such destruction upon it. From generation to generation, the world will remain in peace for all eternity.

Chapter XI

In those days, I will open the great storehouses of blessings in heaven and pour them down onto the earth. These blessings will flow generously, rewarding the hard work of people and enriching their lives. They will not only nourish the land but also bring renewal and prosperity to everyone, filling all of creation with abundance.

Truth and peace will come together in perfect harmony, lasting through every generation. They will be the foundation of life, ensuring that goodness and balance remain forever. This lasting bond between truth and peace will create a world where righteousness thrives, guiding and giving hope to humanity for all time.

Chapter XII

I, Enoch, was giving blessings and praise to the Lord of majesty, the King of all time. As I was doing this, the Watchers called out to me. They spoke to me as Enoch the scribe and said, "Enoch, writer of righteousness, go and deliver a message to the Watchers of heaven—those who left their high and holy home. They have made themselves unclean by taking human wives and acting like the people of the earth.

Tell them, 'You have brought great destruction upon the world. Because of this, you will never find peace, and your sins will never be forgiven. Since you take joy in your children, you will have to watch them die and be destroyed. You will grieve for them and cry out forever, but know this—you will never receive mercy or peace.'"

Chapter XIII

Enoch went to Azâzêl and said, "You will never have peace. A severe judgment has been given against you, and you will be chained. You will not be shown mercy or have your requests granted because of the evil you have taught and the sinful acts you have led people to commit."

Then I went to speak to all of them together, and they were overcome with fear. They trembled in terror and begged me to write a petition for them, hoping they could be forgiven. They wanted me to bring their request before the Lord of heaven.

From that moment, they could no longer speak with Him or even look up toward heaven because they were ashamed of their sins and the punishment they had received. I wrote down their petition, including their prayer about their spirits, their actions, and their plea for forgiveness and a longer life.

I went to sit by the waters of Dan, in the land of Dan, southwest of Mount Hermon. There, I read their petition over and over until I fell asleep.

As I slept, I had a dream and saw visions. I saw punishments being carried out, and a voice called out, telling me to deliver a message to the fallen angels and warn them.

When I woke up, I went to them. They were gathered together, weeping in Abelsjâîl, a place between Lebanon and Sênêsêr. Their faces were filled with shame.

I told them everything I had seen in my dream. Then, I began to speak words of truth and righteousness and rebuked the fallen Watchers for their sins.

Chapter XIV

This book contains words of truth and a warning to the fallen Watchers, as commanded by the Holy Great One in a vision.

While I was asleep, I saw something that I will now share, using the voice and breath given to me by the Great One. He has gifted humanity with speech and understanding so that we can think and communicate. Just as He has given people wisdom, He has also given me the duty to warn the Watchers, the heavenly beings who turned away.

I wrote down your request, but in my vision, I saw that it will not be accepted. Judgment has already been decided, and your plea will never be granted, not now or ever. From this moment on, you will never return to heaven. The decision is final, and you will remain bound to the earth for all time.

You will watch as your beloved sons are destroyed, and there will be no joy left for you. They will die by the sword before your eyes, and your prayers for them will not be heard. Even if you cry out, pray, and repeat every word written in your request, it will not be answered.

Then, in my vision, I saw something incredible: Clouds gathered around me and called me forward, while mist surrounded me. Bright stars and flashes of lightning moved quickly, and powerful winds lifted me, carrying me high into the heavens.

I traveled until I reached a massive crystal wall, surrounded by flames of fire. The sight filled me with fear. I passed through the fire and saw a magnificent house made entirely of crystal. Its walls sparkled like gems, and its foundation was also crystal-clear.

The ceiling of this house looked like the sky filled with stars and lightning, and fiery beings moved between them. The heavens above were as clear as water. A blazing fire surrounded the walls, and the gates of the house glowed with flames.

When I entered, I felt an intense heat, like fire, and at the same time, a deep cold, like ice. There was no comfort inside—only a powerful sense of fear. I trembled and fell on my face.

As I lay there, another vision appeared before me: A second house, even greater and more magnificent than the first, stood open before me. This house was built entirely of fire, and its beauty and size were beyond anything I could describe.

The floor was made of fire, and above it stretched paths of lightning and stars. The ceiling burned with flames. Inside, I saw a high throne that shone like crystal, with wheels as bright as the sun. Around it were visions of heavenly beings.

Beneath the throne, streams of flaming fire flowed so brightly that I could not look at them directly. Seated on the throne was the Great Glory. His robe was brighter than the sun and whiter than any snow. No angel could approach Him because of His overwhelming majesty and brilliance. No living being could look upon His face.

Flames of fire surrounded Him, and a great fire burned before Him. No one could get near Him. Tens of thousands upon thousands stood before Him, yet He needed no advice from anyone. The holiest ones in His presence never left His side, not during the day or the night.

I lay there, trembling, with my face pressed to the ground. Then the Lord Himself spoke, calling my name, "Come here, Enoch, and listen to My words."

One of the holy ones came to me, helped me rise, and led me to the entrance. In deep respect, I bowed my face down before Him.

Chapter XV

Then He answered me, and I heard His voice clearly as He said, "Do not be afraid, Enoch, righteous man and scribe of truth. Come closer and listen carefully to My words.

Go and give this message to the fallen Watchers who sent you to plead for them. It is not humans who should speak on your behalf, but you who should pray for them.

Why did you leave the high and holy heaven? Why did you take human wives and make yourselves unclean with them? You acted like earthly beings and had children with them, creating giants as your sons.

You were once pure and spiritual, living forever, yet you became corrupted by human desires. You gave in to fleshly desires, just like mortal men who are destined to die.

I gave men wives so they could have children and continue life on earth. Their needs would be met, and everything would be provided for them.

But you were different. You were created as spiritual beings, meant to live forever in heaven. That is why I did not give you wives.

The heavenly ones were meant to stay in heaven, not take part in human ways.

Now, the children born from your union with human women will be known as evil spirits on earth, for that is where they belong. These spirits come from both men and fallen angels, and because of their corrupted origin, they will forever be known as wicked spirits.

The spirits of heaven will remain in heaven, but the spirits born on earth must stay on earth, as this is their rightful place.

The spirits of these giants will bring suffering, oppression, and destruction. They will fight against people, cause chaos, and bring misery to the world. They will not eat food, but they will always be hungry and thirsty. They will continue to harm others and spread pain. These spirits will rise against humanity and women because they came from them and are tied to their actions."

Chapter XVI

Since the time when the giants were destroyed, the spirits that came from their bodies have continued to bring destruction without being judged. They will keep doing this until the final day—the great day of judgment—when the world as it is now will come to an end. On that day, judgment will be carried out against the fallen Watchers and the wicked, and everything will be set right.

As for the Watchers who sent you to plead for them—those who once lived in heaven—give them this message: "You once lived in heaven, but not all its secrets were revealed to you. Instead, you only learned things that were useless and harmful. Yet, with stubborn hearts, you taught these things to human women. Because of this knowledge, both men and women have done great evil on the earth."

So tell them this: "You will never have peace."

The Book of Giants
(Fragmented Text)

Introduction

The mysterious figure of Enoch, briefly mentioned in the Book of Genesis, has fascinated scholars and religious thinkers for centuries. The Bible describes him as a man who "walked with God" and was taken by Him (Genesis 5:24), which has inspired many writings that explore his life and the mysteries surrounding him. One of these texts, The Book of Giants, gives a deeper look into the world before the Great Flood, focusing on events involving powerful beings known as the Watchers.

The journey of The Book of Giants from being almost unknown to gaining scholarly attention shows how ancient stories can survive over time. Pieces of this text were first discovered among the Dead Sea Scrolls in the mid-20th century, specifically in caves 1, 2, 4, and 6 at Qumran. These Aramaic fragments, written before the 2nd century BCE, helped connect the short biblical mentions of Enoch with the more detailed stories found in other ancient writings. The discovery highlighted the text's importance in understanding the religious and cultural world of the Second Temple period.

The Book of Giants tells the story of what happened when the "sons of God" came to Earth. These heavenly beings, called the Watchers, formed forbidden relationships with human women, which led to the birth of giant hybrid children known as the Nephilim. These giants, blessed with incredible strength and size, soon became violent rulers, bringing chaos and destruction to the world. The story focuses on two of these giants, Ohyah and Hahyah, the sons of the leader of the Watchers, Shemihaza. Their dreams, later explained by Enoch, warn of a coming disaster as punishment for their actions. The book highlights themes of divine justice and the dangers of breaking the natural order.

Many of the ideas in The Book of Giants are similar to stories from other ancient cultures, especially myths about gods or divine beings having children with humans. The presence of names like Gilgamesh, a well-known figure from Mesopotamian legends, suggests that the book combines elements from different traditions, showing a shared cultural history. The text also adds more details to the biblical story of the Great Flood, explaining that it was not just caused by human evil but also by the chaos created by the Watchers and their children.

Although The Book of Giants was written before the 2nd century BCE, it was kept alive through the Manichaean religion. Manichaeism, a gnostic faith that began in the 3rd century CE, adopted and modified the story, making it part of their religious teachings. Fragments of the book have been found in Turfan, Western China, proving that it was shared across many cultures and remained influential for centuries.

Today, The Book of Giants gives scholars and history enthusiasts a better understanding of early Jewish beliefs, ancient religious writings, and the development of ideas about angels and demons. The stories in this book challenge readers to think about the divide between the human and divine worlds—and what happens when those boundaries are crossed. As we explore this translation, we have the opportunity to reflect on these ancient ideas and what they say about morality, justice, and the human experience.

This version of The Book of Giants aims to stay true to its original meaning while making it easy to read and understand. It keeps the richness of the original text while helping readers see the historical and cultural background that shaped its creation.

Book Of Giants -- Reconstructed Texts

A group of fallen angels came down to Earth, bringing both secret knowledge and destruction.

They learned things they were never supposed to know.
Sin spread everywhere.
They became violent and killed many people.
Their children grew into giants.

The angels used Earth's resources for themselves.

They took everything the land produced.
They ruled over the sea, the sky, and all living things.
They ate the fruit, grain, and trees.
They took animals, from wild beasts to tiny creatures, and watched everything happening on Earth.
They joined in terrible acts, bringing corruption to humanity.

The two hundred fallen angels began experimenting with different creatures, including humans.

They took donkeys, rams, goats, and other animals from the land and sky.
They used them in unnatural ways, mixing them in ways that were never meant to happen.

This corruption led to chaos, violence, and monsters roaming the Earth.
They ruined the world.
They created giants and unnatural creatures.
Their evil spread everywhere.
The Earth was filled with bloodshed, and the giants were never satisfied.

They destroyed everything and devoured whatever they could.
Monsters attacked whatever stood in their way.

The land was torn apart.
Terrifying creatures appeared and grew stronger.
They didn't understand the full impact of their actions.
Their choices made the Earth worse.
The fallen angels' influence caused great destruction.
In the end, everything would collapse because of them.
Yet, even after all this, they were never satisfied.

The giants began having strange dreams and visions. One of them, Mahway, the son of the angel Barakel, had a dream that disturbed him. He saw a tablet placed in water. When it was pulled out, only three names remained while the rest had disappeared. This seemed to warn that almost everyone would be wiped out, leaving only a few survivors—Noah and his family—after a great flood.

A tablet was soaked in water.
The water rose and covered it.
When it was lifted out, most of the names were gone.

Mahway told the other giants about his dream, and they tried to
      understand what it meant.
He realized the vision was a warning of disaster.

He admitted his fear to the others and spoke of the spirits of the
      dead, who cried out for justice against those who had killed
      them.
He saw that they would all die soon, and their time was almost
      up.

Ohya, one of the giants, asked Mahway who had given him this
      vision.
Mahway said his father, Barakel, had been with him.

Before he could finish, Ohya interrupted, shocked by what he had heard.

He shouted, "This is unbelievable! If even a woman who cannot have children gives birth, then something truly impossible is happening."

Ohya spoke to Hahya, saying that destruction was coming to the Earth.

When they realized this, they cried before the giants.

Ohya then told Hahya that it was not their fault, but Azaiel's.

He said the giants were the children of fallen angels, and they would not let their loved ones be abandoned.

He also said they had not been completely defeated, and they still had strength left.

The giants began to understand that they could not win against the powers of Heaven. One of the speakers might have been Gilgamesh.

A giant declared that he was strong, with great power in his arms.

He had fought against mortals and waged war, but he now realized he could not defeat his enemies.

They lived in Heaven, in sacred places, and were far stronger than him.

He had been called a wild beast and a wild man.

Then Ohya spoke and said he had a dream that disturbed him.

It kept him awake and forced him to see a vision.

He now understood something important.

His vision was about a tree being uprooted, except for three roots.

It carried the same message as a previous dream.

As he watched, three roots remained.

Then something moved them into a garden.

Ohya tried to ignore what the vision meant.
At first, he claimed it only referred to the demon Azazel.
Now, he suggested it was only about the rulers of the Earth.

The vision spoke about the fate of their souls.
Ohya told the giants what Gilgamesh had said.
The leader had cursed the rulers, and the giants were pleased by
    his words.
Then he left.

The giants were troubled by more dreams.
Two of them woke up, frightened by what they had seen.
They went to their fellow giants and described their visions.

One of them had dreamed of a garden.
Gardeners were watering trees.
Two hundred trees had large branches growing from their roots.
Then, fire spread and burned the entire garden.

The dreamers went to the giants and told them what they had
    seen.
Someone suggested they should find Enoch to explain the
    meaning of the dreams.

Ohya spoke to the giants and told them about his own dream.
He had seen the Ruler of Heaven come down to Earth.
When he finished, the giants and monsters became terrified.
They called Mahway and asked him to go find Enoch.

Mahway was sent to find Enoch, the wise scribe, to ask him
    about the visions.
He flew through the air like strong winds, moving like an eagle.
He left the land behind and passed through a great desert.

When Enoch saw Mahway, he greeted him.

Mahway told him the giants and monsters were waiting for answers.

They wanted to know what their dreams meant.

Enoch sent back a tablet with a warning.

The message was written in his own hand and was addressed to Shemihaza and his followers.

He warned them about the things they had done.

Their wives and children had followed their wicked ways.

The land itself was crying out against them.

Because of their actions, destruction was coming.

A great flood would wipe out all life on land and sea.

But there was still a chance to change.

They were told to break free from evil and pray.

In another vision, Enoch saw something that filled him with fear.

He collapsed to the ground when he heard a voice.

He saw a being who lived among humans but had not learned from them.

Enoch II
The Book of the Secrets of Enoch
(Slavonic Enoch)

Short Account of The Book

The book known as The Secrets of Enoch has only been preserved in the Slavonic language. To keep things simple, we will call it Slavonic Enoch to distinguish it from an older book of Enoch, which has been fully passed down in the Ethiopic language. For convenience, we will refer to that older text as Ethiopic Enoch.

This newly discovered Enoch text was found in recent times through manuscripts in Russia and Serbia. I first became aware of it while working on the Ethiopic Enoch. In an article by Kozak about Russian Pseudepigraphic Literature (published in 1892), I read that a Slavonic version of the Book of Enoch existed, even though only the Ethiopic version had been known before. I quickly reached out to Mr. Morfill for help, and within a few weeks, we obtained printed copies of two of the manuscripts mentioned. After careful study, we realized that Kozak's claim was incorrect.

Instead of being just another version of the Ethiopic Enoch, The Secrets of Enoch turned out to be an entirely different book. However, it is just as important in many ways. Slavonic Enoch was written around the beginning of the Christian era, and its author (or final editor) was a Hellenistic Jew. The book was composed in Egypt.

Because of when and where it was written, it likely did not have a direct impact on the writers of the New Testament. However, its language and ideas are surprisingly similar to some parts of the New

Testament, even helping to explain certain difficult passages. Although knowledge of this book was lost for nearly 1,200 years, it was widely read by early Christians and even some groups considered heretical.

Some sections of this book, though often not credited, appear in other ancient writings, such as the Book of Adam and Eve, the Apocalypses of Moses and Paul (written around 400–500 AD), the Sibylline Oracles, the Ascension of Isaiah, and the Epistle of Barnabas (written around 70–90 AD). It is even mentioned by name in the apocalyptic sections of the Testaments of Levi, Daniel, and Naphtali (around 1 AD). Origen referred to it, and it was likely known by Clement of Alexandria and used by Irenaeus. Some phrases from the New Testament may have even been influenced by it.

The Slavonic Manuscripts

The Slavonic version of the Book of Enoch has been translated into English for the first time here. It exists in two main versions, both of which come from a lost Greek original. The surviving manuscripts can be grouped into different categories.

The first category includes complete versions of the text. Two such manuscripts exist. One, owned by Mr. A. Khludov, is a South Russian version from the late 1600s. It is part of a collection containing religious writings, including the lives of saints. Mr. A. Popov published this text in 1880 in the Transactions of the Historical and Archaeological Society of the University of Moscow. However, this manuscript contains many errors. While it serves as the foundation for this translation, I have made corrections using other sources. In this translation, it is labeled as "A."

Another complete manuscript was discovered in 1886 by Professor Sokolov of Moscow in the Public Library of Belgrade. This version is Bulgarian, with a writing style typical of Middle

Bulgarian, and it likely dates to the 1500s. It contains extra material, including stories about Methuselah's priesthood, Nir, Melchizedek's birth, and the Great Flood. These additions are not originally part of the Book of Enoch but appear as an appendix.

There is also a shorter and incomplete version of the text, known from three manuscripts. One is housed in the Public Library of Belgrade, a Serbian version published by Novakovic in 1884 in the 16th volume of the literary magazine Starine. This manuscript, dating to the 1500s, has some unique readings and is referred to as "B" in this translation. Another similar manuscript is kept in the Vienna Public Library, and a third, from the 1600s, belongs to Mr. E. Barsov of Moscow.

Of these manuscripts, I have direct access only to "A" and "B." My understanding of the others comes from Professor Sokolov's edited text, which includes all the manuscripts. However, his edition does not clearly separate them. To avoid confusion, I refer to his combined text as "Sok," meaning it represents all sources other than "A" and "B."

Additional fragments of the Book of Enoch can be found in Tikhonravov's Memorials of Russian Apocryphal Literature and Pypin's Memorials of Old Russian Literature. References in early Slavonic writings suggest that these later manuscripts are copies of much older ones that no longer exist. For example, Tikhonravov mentions a manuscript from the 1300s.

My main goal as a translator has been to create a version useful to Western scholars studying apocryphal literature. I have not focused on linguistic details, so my Slavonic colleagues should not criticize me for avoiding in-depth language analysis. That type of study is not yet a priority in England. Instead, my translation aims to support my friend, the Rev. R. H. Charles, so he can explore this subject more thoroughly in relation to Biblical apocryphal literature.

I would also like to thank Professors Sokolov and Pavlov of the University of Moscow. Professor Sokolov kindly let me use his revised text and provided helpful notes on difficult sections. Professor Pavlov has shown great interest in this work, and I am grateful for his support. With the help of Mr. Charles and others, I am happy to have made a small contribution to this field of study.

The Son of Ared;
A Man Wise and Beloved of God

[Concerning the Life and the Dream of Enoch]

There was once a very wise man who achieved great things. God loved him deeply and chose him to see the heavenly realms, the places of wisdom, and the eternal, unchanging God. He was shown the Lord of all—glorious, bright, and beyond imagination. He saw the shining presence of God's servants, the throne that no one can approach, and the countless spiritual beings who serve the Lord. He witnessed their different forms, heard their indescribable songs, and saw the vastness of the universe.

At that time, he said, "When I was 165 years old, my son Methuselah was born. After that, I lived another 200 years, making my total lifespan 365 years."

On the first day of the first month, I was alone in my house. I lay down on my bed and fell asleep. As I slept, a deep sadness filled my heart, and I began to weep in my dream. I didn't understand why I was feeling this way or what was about to happen to me.

Then, two men appeared before me. They were very tall, unlike any humans I had ever seen. Their faces shone like the sun, their eyes burned like torches, and fire came from their mouths. Their clothes looked like they were made of feathers, their feet glowed purple, and their wings were brighter than gold. Their hands were as white as snow. They stood by my bed and called me by my name.

I woke up and saw them clearly standing in front of me. I was terrified and quickly bowed before them. My face changed because of the fear I felt.

The men said to me, "Do not be afraid, Enoch. Be strong. The eternal God has sent us to you. Today, you will go with us into heaven."

They continued, "Tell your sons, your servants, and everyone in your household not to search for you until the Lord returns you to them."

I quickly did as they said and left my house. I called my sons—Methuselah, Regim, and Gaidal—and told them everything these two men had said to me.

Chapters I. 2 II.2

Listen to me, my children, because I do not know where I am going or what will happen to me. I ask you now, my children, do not turn away from God. Stay faithful to the Lord and follow His ways. Do not worship useless idols that did not create the heavens and the earth, because they will be destroyed along with those who follow them.

May God give you strength to remain faithful and always respect Him. And now, my children, do not search for me until the Lord returns me to you.

After I finished speaking to my sons, the two men who had appeared to me called me to them. They lifted me up on their wings and placed me on the clouds. The clouds began to rise, carrying me higher and higher.

As I ascended, I looked down and saw the air far below me. As we went even higher, I entered a new place beyond the sky. The men brought me to the first heaven, where they showed me a vast and powerful sea—much larger than any sea on earth.

Chapters II.3VII. 1

They brought me before the elders and leaders in charge of the stars, showing me two hundred angels who guide the stars and make sure they follow their paths in the sky. These angels had wings and moved in circles around the stars, keeping them in their correct places.

Then I looked and saw huge storehouses filled with snow and ice, guarded by angels who watched over these powerful treasures. I also saw where the clouds were kept, the place where they form and where they return.

Next, they showed me the storehouses of the dew, which looked like a fine, anointing oil. Its colors were as beautiful and varied as all the colors on earth. Many angels were assigned to guard these places, opening and closing them at the right times.

The men who were guiding me then took me to the second heaven. There, I saw a dark and dreadful place where prisoners were hanging, waiting for eternal judgment. These angels were filled with sorrow and despair, darker than the deepest shadow on earth. They cried out constantly, their voices filled with pain.

I asked the men with me, "Why are these beings suffering endlessly?" They answered, "These are the ones who turned away from the Lord. They refused to follow His commands and chose their own ways instead. They rebelled with their leader, and now they are imprisoned here in the second heaven."

I felt deep pity for them. Then, to my surprise, the angels turned toward me, bowed, and said, "Man of God, pray to the Lord for us." But I answered, "Who am I, a mere human, to pray for angels? I don't even know where I am going or what will happen to me. I don't even know who could pray for me."

Chapers VI I. 2V III. 5

[Of the taking of Enoch to the third Heaven 2.]

The men then took me to the third heaven. They placed me in the middle of a breathtaking garden, a place more beautiful than anything I had ever seen.

I saw trees of every color, full of ripe, sweet-smelling fruit that filled the air with a wonderful fragrance. There was an endless supply of food, each kind giving off its own pleasant scent.

At the center of the garden stood the Tree of Life, where God Himself rests when He visits Paradise. This tree was beyond words, its beauty unmatched. It gave off a heavenly fragrance, and its appearance shone like gold, deep red, and something like glowing fire, radiating light all around.

From its roots, four streams flowed—one of honey, one of milk, one of oil, and one of wine. These streams moved gently, spreading out in four directions. They flowed toward the Paradise of Eden, existing between the worlds of the living and the eternal, and continued their course across the earth, moving in harmony with the rest of creation.

There was also an olive tree that never stopped producing oil. Every tree in this garden bore fruit, and each one was overflowing with blessings.

Three hundred glorious angels guarded the garden, singing songs of praise without end. Their voices filled the air, offering worship to the Lord every day. I was amazed by the beauty of this place and said, "What an incredibly blessed place this is!" The men who were with me answered.

Chapters VIII. 6X. 2

[The showing to Enoch of the Righteous, and the Place of Prayer]

"This place, Enoch, has been prepared for the righteous. It is for those who have endured many hardships and attacks in their lives, yet have remained strong. It is for those who turn away from evil and choose to do what is right. It belongs to those who feed the hungry, clothe those in need, help the weak, and care for orphans who have no one to protect them. It is for those who live blamelessly before the Lord and serve Him with all their hearts. This is their eternal reward, a place of peace prepared just for them."

Then the men took me to the northern side, where I saw a place so terrifying that words could not describe it. It was filled with unbearable suffering. Thick darkness covered everything, and it was impossible to see through the heavy gloom. There was no light, only a fierce and never-ending fire. A river of flames flowed through it without stopping. The entire place was surrounded by burning fire, yet at the same time, there were icy winds and freezing cold. It was a place of both unbearable heat and bitter cold.

Inside this terrible place were prisoners who looked wild and tormented. The angels guarding them were fierce and showed no mercy. They carried terrifying weapons and punished the prisoners without relief. I cried out, "Oh no! This place is horrifying!"

The men with me answered, "This place, Enoch, is for those who have rejected God and lived wickedly on earth.

"It is for those who have committed terrible sins, practiced witchcraft, and used dark magic. It is for those who took pride in their evil actions, stole from others, spread lies, and caused harm out of jealousy. It is for those who lived in impurity, committed murder, and took advantage of the weak.

"This place belongs to those who let the hungry starve when they could have fed them and left the poor without clothing when they had the power to help. It is for those who did not acknowledge their Creator but instead worshiped idols—lifeless objects that cannot see or hear. These false gods were made by human hands, yet they bowed down to them as if they had power.

"For all these people, this place has been prepared as their eternal punishment."

Chapters X.3XI.1

[Here they took Enoch to the fourth Heaven, where is the Course of the Sun and Moon.]

The men then took me to the fourth heaven, where they showed me how the sun and moon move along their paths. I saw how bright their light was and measured their courses. I learned that the sun's light is seven times stronger than the moon's. I watched as they traveled in their orbits, moving quickly like a rushing wind. They never stopped, continuing their journey day and night without rest.

I saw four large stars moving alongside the sun. Each of these stars had a thousand smaller stars following on its right side, and another four stars had a thousand stars each on their left side. In total, there were eight thousand stars surrounding the sun.

Around the sun, I saw an enormous group of angels—fifteen myriads of them—who traveled with it during the day, guiding and watching over it. At night, a thousand angels took their place to accompany it.

Each of these angels had six wings, and they flew in front of the sun's chariot, leading and directing its path. A hundred other angels were given the task of keeping the sun warm and bright, making sure its light and heat reached the earth. It was an incredible sight, a breathtaking display of heavenly order and divine power.

Chapters XI. 2—XII.I

[Of the wonderful Creatures of the Sun.]

I looked and saw amazing flying creatures, unlike anything I had ever seen before. They were called phoenixes and chalkadri, and their appearance was both incredible and strange. These creatures had the feet and tails of lions, but their heads looked like crocodiles. Their bodies shimmered with a purple glow, shining like a bright rainbow. Each one was enormous, measuring nine hundred units in size.

They had wings like angels, with twelve large and powerful wings each. These creatures served the sun's chariot, traveling alongside it on its journey. They carried out tasks given to them by God, bringing heat and dew to the earth as commanded.

As the sun moved along its path, these creatures followed, guiding its way beneath the sky and through the hidden places under the earth. The sun's light never stopped shining, constantly moving to brighten the world and sustain life below.

Chapters XII. 2XIII. 5

[The Angels took Enoch, and placed him on the East at the Gates of the Sun.]

The men took me to the East, where they showed me the gates through which the sun rises at different times. The sun follows a set pattern based on the changing seasons, the months of the year, and the hours of day and night.

I saw six enormous gates, each carefully measured. They were massive, with each gate measuring sixty-one stadia and a quarter of a stadium. I measured them myself and confirmed their enormous size. These gates are where the sun begins its journey, moving westward and following a path that changes with the months and seasons.

The sun travels through the first gate for forty-two days, then through the second gate for thirty-five days. It moves through the fourth and fifth gates for thirty-five days each. However, when it passes through the sixth gate, it stays there for forty-five days.

After that, the sun reverses its path, returning from the sixth gate. It moves through the fifth gate for thirty-five days, then the fourth gate for thirty-five days, followed by the third gate for thirty-five days, and finally through the second gate for another thirty-five days.

This completes the full year, with all the days perfectly matching the sun's cycle and the changes in the four seasons.

Chapters XIV. 1XV. 4

[They took Enock to the West.]

The men then took me to the western part of the sky and showed me six huge open gates. These gates were just like the ones in the East, and through them, the sun sets after completing its journey across the 365 days and a quarter of a day in a year.

As the sun passes through the Western gates, 400 angels come to take its crown and bring it before the Lord. The sun, traveling in its chariot, remains without its light for seven full hours during the night. But when it reaches the East during the eighth hour, the 400 angels return its crown and place it back on the sun.

At that moment, the Phoenixes and Chalkidri, special creatures of the sun, begin to sing. Because of their song, all the birds in the world flap their wings with joy, praising the giver of light. These creatures sing at the Lord's command.

The sun then rises again, spreading its light across the entire earth. The men explained to me how the sun's movements are measured and showed me the gates through which it enters and exits. These great gates were designed by God to mark the passing of days and to set the cycle of the year.

This is why the sun is so large and plays such an important role in the order of the world.

Chapter XVI.17

[The Men· took Enoch and placed him at the East, at the Course of the Moon.]

The men then explained to me how the moon's movements are calculated. They showed me its paths and cycles, pointing out twelve large gates stretching from west to east. The moon enters and exits through these gates at its set times.

The moon moves through the first gate when the sun is in the west, staying there for exactly thirty-one days. It also spends thirty-one days in the second gate. In the third and fourth gates, it remains for thirty days each. It continues this pattern, staying in the fifth and sixth gates for thirty-one days, in the seventh gate for thirty days, in the eighth and ninth gates for thirty-one days, in the tenth gate for thirty days, in the eleventh for thirty-one days, and in the twelfth for twenty-eight days. This cycle repeats as the moon moves through the western gates, following the same pattern as the eastern gates, completing the year.

The sun's yearly cycle is 365 days and a quarter, but the lunar year is only 354 days, made up of twelve months of twenty-nine days each. This leaves an extra eleven days that must be added to match the sun's full cycle for the year. These additional days, called lunar epacts, make up the difference between the sun and the moon's cycles.

Over three years, the extra quarter day from each year is ignored, but in the fourth year, the missing time is accounted for. That is why three years seem to be missing days, but in the fourth year, everything aligns again. To keep the calculations correct, two extra months are added over time, while others are slightly adjusted to maintain balance.

Once the moon completes its cycle through the western gates, it returns to the eastern gates, bringing its light. It moves constantly, both day and night, traveling along its set path faster than the winds of the sky. Alongside it are spirits, creatures, and angels, each with six wings, who guide its movements.

Seven months of the moon's cycle are also measured within a larger cycle of nineteen years, ensuring that everything in the sky stays in perfect order.

Chapters XVI. 8XVIII. 3

In the middle of the heavens, I saw a vast army of angels, armed and ready to serve the Lord. They played cymbals and organs, and their voices rose in endless songs of praise. The sound was unlike anything I had ever heard—so beautiful and powerful that it stirred my soul with joy.

Then, the men guiding me led me further and took me up to the fifth heaven. There, I saw an enormous crowd, too many to count. These were the Grigori, and while they looked like men, they were much larger, even bigger than giants.

Their faces looked tired and sorrowful, and they were completely silent. The entire place felt heavy and lifeless—there was no worship, no joy, and no service to the Lord. Confused, I turned to the men who brought me there and asked, "Why do these beings look so sad and lifeless? Why are they silent, and why is there no worship here?"

They answered, "These are the Grigori. Long ago, they and their leader, Satanail, turned away from the Lord. Because of their rebellion, they were cast into great darkness in the second heaven. Three of them were sent down from God's throne to a place called Ermon. There, at Mount Iermon, they saw the daughters of men, found them beautiful, and took them as wives.

By doing this, they disobeyed God and brought corruption to the earth. They abandoned their duties and went against His will. Their children became giants, men of great size and strength, but their existence only brought wickedness and chaos. Sin and lawlessness spread everywhere because of them.

Because of their actions, God passed a severe judgment on them. Now, they mourn for their fallen brothers, knowing they will face punishment on the great and terrible day of the Lord."

Hearing this, I turned to the Grigori and said, "I have seen what happened to your brothers and the suffering they endure. I prayed for them, but the Lord has decided they must remain trapped under the earth until the heavens and the earth pass away. They will never be set free."

I continued, "Why are you waiting, my brothers? Why do you not serve before the Lord? Why do you not fulfill your duties and give Him the honor He deserves instead of continuing in your rebellion?"

When I finished speaking, the Grigori listened to my words. They arranged themselves into four groups within the heaven. As I stood with the men who guided me, four trumpets sounded together, filling the air with a deep and powerful sound. Then, the Grigori began to sing as one. Their voices were filled with sorrow, but their song was soft and moving. Their mournful song rose up before the Lord, carrying their regret and longing for redemption.

Chapters XVIII. 4XIX. 2

[The taking up of Enoch, i1tto the sixth, Heaven.]

The men guiding me then took me further and brought me to the sixth heaven. There, I saw seven groups of angels, each one glowing with incredible brightness. Their faces shone even brighter than the sun's rays, and their beauty was beyond anything I had ever seen. They all looked the same, with no differences in their appearance, expressions, or clothing. They stood together in perfect unity.

These angels were responsible for studying and organizing the movements of the stars, the phases of the moon, and the paths of the sun. They ensured that balance was kept in the world, controlling both good and bad conditions as they had been commanded. They also arranged teachings and instructions and created beautiful songs and melodies filled with praise and glory.

These angels were archangels, the leaders over all the other angels. They had authority over everything, both in heaven and on earth. Some were in charge of keeping track of the changing seasons and the passing of years. Others watched over the rivers and seas, making sure the waters flowed as they should. There were also angels who oversaw the growth of plants and trees, ensuring that all living creatures received the food they needed.

I also saw angels who were responsible for recording the lives and actions of every person on earth. They carefully wrote down everything before the Lord, making sure that no deed—good or bad—was ever forgotten.

In the middle of these angels, I saw seven phoenixes, seven cherubim, and seven other beings with six wings each. Together, they sang in perfect harmony with one voice. Their song was so beautiful and powerful that words could not describe it. It was a joyful offering to the Lord, rising up to His holy throne as a tribute to His greatness and glory.

Chapters XIX. 3—XX. 3

[Thence Enoch is taken into the seventh. Heaven]

The men guiding me took me even higher, bringing me to the seventh heaven. There, I saw a breathtaking and brilliant light. Surrounding it were powerful archangels, spirits of great strength, rulers, and other mighty beings. I saw cherubim and seraphim, shining thrones, and countless watchful eyes. In front of me stood ten groups of radiant beings, each more dazzling than the last. The sight was so overwhelming that I trembled in fear, unable to fully comprehend what I was seeing.

Sensing my fear, the men with me held me and reassured me, saying, "Do not be afraid, Enoch. Be at peace." Their words comforted me, and I was able to stand among them.

Then, they showed me the Lord from a distance, seated on His magnificent and exalted throne. His presence was beyond words—majestic and awe-inspiring. Around Him, all the heavenly beings were gathered, each standing on one of ten steps, perfectly arranged according to their rank. They bowed before the Lord, showing Him deep reverence and honor.

After paying their respects, they returned to their places. With joy and devotion, they stood in the endless light of His presence. In soft and harmonious voices, they sang praises, glorifying the Lord and serving Him with love and honor in the brilliance of His unending glory.

Chapters XX. 4—XXII. 5

[How the Angels placed Enoch there at the limits of the seventh Heaven and departed from him invisibly.]

They never leave, day or night, but remain before the Lord, carrying out His commands. Surrounding His throne are the cherubim and seraphim, along with six-winged beings who cover His throne with their presence. They sing softly, their voices full of reverence, proclaiming, "Holy, Holy, Holy, Lord God of Hosts! Heaven and earth are filled with Your glory!"

After witnessing these incredible things, the men who had guided me turned to me and said, "Enoch, our task is complete." Then they departed, leaving me alone. Standing at the edge of heaven, fear overtook me. I fell on my face, trembling, and cried out in distress, "What is happening to me?"

But the Lord, in His mercy, sent one of His great archangels—Gabriel. Gabriel spoke gently to me, saying, "Be at peace, Enoch. Do not be afraid. Stand up and follow me, for you will always remain before the Lord." Though his words were meant to calm me, I answered, "O Lord, my spirit is overwhelmed with fear. Please send back the men who brought me here. They were my companions, and with them, I would feel safe to approach You."

Gabriel, however, swiftly lifted me as if I were a leaf carried by the wind. He brought me directly before the Lord. Overcome with awe, I fell on my face and worshiped Him. Then the Lord Himself spoke to me, saying, "Be at peace, Enoch. Do not fear. Stand before Me, for you will remain in My presence forever."

Then Michael, the chief of the archangels, approached and lifted me up. He presented me before the Lord, and the Lord commanded His heavenly servants, "Let Enoch stand before Me forever." The glorious beings bowed low before the Lord and answered, "Let it be done according to Your word, O Lord."

Then the Lord turned to Michael and said, "Remove Enoch's earthly garments and anoint him with My holy oil. Then clothe him in the robe of My glory." Michael obeyed. He took away my earthly robe and anointed me with oil that shone brighter than the sun. The oil smelled sweeter than the finest myrrh, felt cool like morning dew, and glowed with brilliant light. Then he dressed me in garments that radiated with divine glory.

As I looked at myself, I saw that I had been transformed. I was now like the glorious beings who serve the Lord, and all fear and trembling left me.

Then the Lord called upon another archangel, Vretil, who was known for his wisdom and for recording all of the Lord's works. The Lord said to him, "Bring the books from My storehouses and give Enoch a reed to write. Teach him the knowledge contained in these books."

Vretil obeyed immediately, bringing books that smelled of myrrh and handing me a reed. With patience and wisdom, he prepared to teach me the mysteries written within those sacred texts.

Chapters XXII. 6—XXIII. 4

[Of the writing of Enoch how he wrote about his wonderful Goings and the heavenly Visions, and he himself wrote 366 Book.]

He showed me how the heavens, the earth, and the seas work. He explained the movement of their elements, the rumble of thunder, the paths of the sun and moon, and the way the stars travel and change. He described the cycles of the seasons and years, the passage of days and hours, the way the winds move, the countless angels in heaven, and the beautiful songs they sing in perfect harmony.

He also revealed everything about people—their lives, their different languages, the songs they sing, their knowledge, and the lessons they follow. He shared the melodies of their voices and all the wisdom they need to understand.

For thirty days and thirty nights, Vretil taught me without stopping, speaking the entire time. And for those same thirty days and nights, I wrote without resting, recording everything he told me.

Then, when the time came, Vretil said to me, "You have written everything I have taught you. Now, write about the souls of all people—the souls that have not yet been born and the places that have been prepared for them for eternity. Every soul was created to live forever, even before the world was made."

I obeyed, writing without stopping for another thirty days and nights. By the time I finished, I had written 366 books, carefully recording everything I had seen and learned.

Chapters XXIII. S—XXIV. 5

[Of the great Secrets of God, Which God revealed and told to Enoch, and spoke with him Face to Face.]

The Lord called me and said, "Enoch, sit at My left side with Gabriel." I bowed down in deep respect before Him.

Then the Lord spoke again, saying, "Enoch, everything you see—whether still or moving—was created by Me. Now, I will show you how I made everything from nothing and how the visible world came from the unseen.

Even My angels do not know these secrets. I have not told them how creation began, and they do not understand the endless greatness of My works, which I am revealing to you today.

Before anything existed, I alone moved through the unseen, just as the sun moves across the sky from east to west. But unlike the sun, which has a place to rest, I never stopped, for I was constantly creating. I shaped the foundation of everything and began to bring visible things into being."

Then the Lord continued, "I commanded the deep abyss so that things could emerge from the invisible. From this unseen realm, Adoil appeared before Me—vast and magnificent, glowing with a brilliant red light.

I said to Adoil, 'Break open, and let what is inside you be seen.' He obeyed, and a great light burst forth. I was surrounded by this brilliant light, and from within it, the entire world was revealed, just as I had planned. I saw that it was good.

Then I made a throne for Myself and sat upon it. I commanded the light, 'Rise high and become the foundation for everything above.' The light obeyed, ascending to the highest place. As I sat on My throne, I looked at the light and marveled at how great it was."

Chapters XXV. 1XXVII. 1

[God again calls from the Depths and there came
Arkhas, Tazhis, and one who is very red.]

I called out again into the emptiness and said, "Let something solid and visible come from what cannot be seen." In response, Arkhas appeared—thick, heavy, and glowing with a deep red color.

I told Arkhas, "Separate, and let what comes from you be seen." When he split apart, a vast and shadowy world was revealed—huge, dark, and endless—bringing the beginning of everything below.

I saw that this was good. I commanded, "Go down and become the base for all that will be beneath." And so it happened. Arkhas sank, became firm, and formed the foundation for everything below. Beyond this darkness, there was nothing more.

Chapters XXVII. 2XXIX. 3

[How God established the Water, and surrounded it with
Light, and established upon it Seven Islands.]

I commanded the light and darkness to be separated and said, "Let there be something thick and solid." And so it appeared. I spread this new substance out, forming water beneath the light, covering the darkness below.

I made the waters firm, shaping the deep places, and surrounded them with light. Then, I created seven layers, making them clear and strong—both smooth and rough—like glass and ice. I set paths for the waters and other elements, guiding them to move in harmony with the seven stars, each within its own part of the sky. I saw that this was good.

I separated light from darkness and divided the waters above from those below. I told the light, "You will be called day," and the darkness, "You will be called night." And so, the first day began with evening and ended with morning.

Next, I made the heavenly layers stronger and gathered the waters below into one place, keeping the waves under control. From these waves, I formed large, solid stones, and from the stones, I shaped dry land, which I named earth. At the center of this land, I created a deep, endless pit.

I brought the sea together in one place and set a boundary for it, saying, "This is where you will stay forever. You will not cross the limits I have set for you." Then, I made the sky firm and placed it above the waters. This was the end of the first day.

When evening and morning passed, the second day began.

For the heavenly beings, I gave them a nature like fire. I looked at a strong, unbreakable stone, and from the brightness of My eye, I gave lightning its powerful glow. I placed fire within the water and water within the fire, making sure that neither would destroy the other. That is why lightning shines brighter than the sun, and soft water can wear down the hardest stone.

From the stone, I brought forth powerful fire, and from this fire, I created countless spiritual beings—ten thousand angels, each armed with weapons of flame and robes of burning light. I commanded them to take their places and follow the purpose I had set for them.

Chapters XXIX. 4XXX. 3

[Here Satanail was hurled from the Heights with his Angels.]

One of the archangels, leading those beneath him, had a thought that could never come true—he wanted to raise his throne above the clouds and have the same power as Me. Because of this, I cast him down from the heights, along with his followers. Now, he wanders endlessly in the air above the abyss.

With that, I finished creating all the heavens, completing the third day. On this day, I commanded the earth to grow tall, fruit-bearing trees, towering mountains, and every kind of plant and seed. I also created Paradise, surrounding it with a protective barrier and placing fiery, armed angels at its entrance to guard it and keep it forever renewed.

When evening passed and morning arrived, it was the fourth day. On this day, I decorated the sky with great lights. In the highest circle, I placed the star Kruno. In the second, I set Aphrodite; in the third, Ares; in the fourth, the Sun; in the fifth, Zeus; in the sixth, Hermes; and in the seventh, the Moon.

I filled the sky below with countless smaller stars, making the Sun shine during the day and the Moon and stars glow at night. I gave the Sun its path through the signs of the Zodiac and set the Moon to follow the same twelve signs. I fixed their names, their purpose, and the timing of their movements—even the sounds of thunder and the precise passing of time.

When evening passed and morning arrived, the fifth day began. On this day, I commanded the sea to be filled with all kinds of fish and winged creatures. I also brought forth crawling creatures, four-legged animals, and everything that moves through the air. Each one was made male and female, given breath and life.

Finally, evening passed and morning arrived, marking the sixth day. On this day, I turned to My Wisdom and directed it to create man, forming him from seven elements.

Chapter XXX. 48

I shaped his body from the earth.
I made his blood from the morning dew.
His eyes came from the light of the sun.
His bones were formed with the strength of stones.
His thoughts were drawn from the speed of angels and the
    drifting clouds.
His veins and hair grew from the grass of the land.
And his spirit came from My own breath and the wind itself.
I gave him seven unique abilities:

His body could hear, his eyes could see, his mind could recognize scents, his veins could feel touch, his blood could taste, his bones could endure, and his thoughts carried both sweetness and wisdom.

I designed man with a perfect balance of what is seen and unseen. His life and death, his shape and spirit, all connected to both realms. Though his creation was small compared to My endless power, it carried a great and deep purpose.

I placed him on the earth as a being like no other, almost like an angel in human form. I gave him honor, strength, and glory.

I made him ruler over the earth, guiding it with My wisdom. Among all that I created, nothing else was like him.

Chapter XXX. 915

I gave him a name inspired by the four directions—East, West, North, and South.

I placed four guiding stars for him and named him Adam.

I gave him free will and showed him two paths—the path of light and the path of darkness. I told him, "This is good, and this is bad," so that his choices would reveal his heart. Through him, his descendants would also show their true nature, whether they loved Me or turned away.

Even though I understood his nature, he did not yet understand himself. This lack of knowledge became his struggle, leading him to make mistakes. Because of his wrongdoing, I declared that death would be the price to pay.

I put him into a deep sleep, and while he slept, I took one of his ribs and created a companion—his wife.

Through her, death entered the world, and I accepted what would become of his descendants. I gave her a name, calling her the mother of all living—Eve.

Chapter XXX. 16, 17

[Goel gives Paradise to Adam, and gives him Knowledge, so as to see the Heavens open, and that he should see the Angels singing a Song if Triumph.]

Adam lived his life on earth, and I created a garden in Eden, in the East, for him. I gave him the responsibility to follow My instructions and care for what I had given him.

I opened the heavens so he could see the angels singing songs of victory. In Paradise, there was always light—no darkness existed there.

But the devil, filled with jealousy, wanted a world of his own because everything on earth was under Adam's rule.

The devil, an evil spirit from the lowest places, became known as Satan after leaving heaven. Before his fall, his name was Satanail.

Though his nature changed, making him different from the angels, he still knew the difference between right and wrong. He fully understood the judgment against him and the sin he had committed.

Out of spite, he plotted against Adam and tricked Eve. But he never directly controlled or touched Adam.

Because of his evil plans, I cursed him for his arrogance and wickedness. However, I did not curse those I had already blessed.

I did not curse man, the earth, or anything I had created. Instead, I cursed the results of man's disobedience and the corruption that came from it.

Chapters XXX. 18XXXIII.1

[On account of the Sin of Adam, God sends him to the Earth, 'From which I took thee,' but He does not wish to destroy him in the Life to come.]

I told him, "You were made from the earth, and one day, you will return to it. I will not destroy you, but you will go back to where you came from. Then, when I return, I will take you again."

I blessed everything I created, both seen and unseen.

I also blessed the seventh day, the Sabbath, because on that day, I rested from all My work.

Chapter XXXIII. 26

[God shows Enoch the Duration of this World, 7000 Years, and the eighth Thousand is the End. (There will be) no Tears, no months, no Weeks, no. Days.]

Then I established the eighth day, making it the first after all My work was done. Let this day represent a time without end—no more counting years, months, weeks, days, or hours, but an everlasting age beyond measure.

Now, Enoch, everything I have told you, all that you have seen in heaven and on earth, and everything you have written—know that I created it all with My wisdom. From the highest places to the lowest, from the beginning to the end, I designed everything. No one advises Me or shares in My work, for I am eternal and not made by anyone. My thoughts never change, My wisdom guides Me, and My word is always true. I see all things, and when I look upon them, they remain as they are. But if I turn away, all things depend on Me to exist.

Listen carefully, Enoch, and understand who is speaking to you. Take the books you have written, for I will send you back with Samuil and Raguil, who brought you here. Return to the earth and tell your sons everything I have revealed to you—all that you have seen, from the lowest heaven to My throne.

I created all the heavenly beings and powers, and none stand against Me or disobey My will. Everything follows My command and exists under My authority. Give your writings to your sons, and they will read them and understand that I am the Creator of all things. They will know there is no other God besides Me.

Your writings will be passed down through their children, spreading across generations and nations. I will send you, Enoch, with My messenger, the great leader Michael, to keep these writings safe alongside the records of your ancestors—Adam, Seth, Enos, Kainan, Mahalaleel, and your father Jared.

These writings will not be needed until the final age. For this reason, I have assigned two angels, Arinkh and Parinkh, to guard them on earth. They will make sure that the story of what happens to your family is not lost when the great flood comes.

Chapters XXXIII. 7XXXV. 1

[God accu.1es the Idolators; the Workers of Iniquity, such as Sodom, and on this account, He brings the Deluge upon them.]

I know how corrupt people will become. They will refuse to follow the path I set for them or use the gifts I have given. Instead, they will reject My guidance, follow another way, and invest in things that have no value. They will worship false gods and turn away from Me, the one true God.

The earth will be filled with evil, wickedness, and impurity. People will harm one another in terrible ways, committing sins too awful to name. Because of this, I will bring a great flood to wipe out everything, for the world will have become completely corrupt.

But I will save one righteous man from your family line, along with his household, because they will follow My ways. Over time, their descendants will grow into a large nation, though many among them will be consumed by their own selfish desires.

When their time ends, I will reveal to them the books you have written, along with the writings of your ancestors. The keepers of these books on earth will share them with those who are faithful to Me—those who respect My name and do not dishonor it. These people will pass the knowledge to the next generation, and those who read it will bring Me even greater glory.

Now, Enoch, I am giving you thirty more days to stay on earth and teach your family. Gather your sons and relatives before Me so they may hear your words. Let them read and understand that there is no other God but Me. Teach them to obey My commandments always and study the books you have written.

After thirty days, I will send My angels to take you away from the earth and from your sons, just as I have planned.

Chapters XXXV.2 XXXIX. 1

[Here God summons an Angel.]

The angel standing beside me was a sight both breathtaking and terrifying. His appearance was as pure as freshly fallen snow, and his hands felt as cold as ice. The chill from his presence sank deep into my face, overwhelming me, for I could not bear the immense power of the Lord. It was like trying to withstand the heat of a blazing fire or the biting cold of the harshest winter.

Then the Lord said to me, "Enoch, if your face does not grow cold in this place, no human on earth could ever look at it and survive."

Meanwhile, my son Mathusal waited with hope, keeping watch by my bedside day and night, longing for my return. The Lord spoke to the ones who had taken me and commanded, "Return Enoch to the earth and remain with him until the appointed time." That night, they brought me back to my bed, where Mathusal had been keeping faithful watch. When he heard me return, he was filled with fear. I called for my whole household to gather because I had much to tell them.

With sorrow in my heart and tears in my eyes, I spoke to my children, filled with deep sadness.

"Listen carefully, my children, to the words given to me by the Lord. Today, I have been sent to you by Him to tell you what has happened, what is happening now, and what will take place before the day of judgment.

"Pay close attention, for these words are not my own. They come directly from the Lord, who has commanded me to share them with you. I am only a man, like you, but I have seen the face of the Lord. It was like metal glowing red-hot in a fire, sending out sparks that burned everything in their path."

"Look into my eyes, the eyes of a man who has been sent to deliver this message. I have looked into the eyes of the Lord, eyes that shine like the sun and fill the hearts of men with fear. Look at my hands, made of flesh like yours. I have seen the right hand of the Lord, a hand so powerful it stretches across the heavens, bringing help and support."

"My actions are human, just like yours, but I have seen the boundless, perfect form of the Lord, a form without limit or measure. You hear my voice, but I have heard the voice of the Lord. His words thunder like a storm, rolling through the sky with the power of roaring clouds."

"My children, listen to the words of your father. You know how terrifying it is to stand before a ruler on earth, knowing that your life or death depends on their judgment. But how much more fearsome, how much more overwhelming, is it to stand before the face of the Lord of all lords, the Master of heaven and earth? Who among us could ever endure such endless fear and trembling?"

Chapters XXXIX. 2XL. 6

[Enoch instructs fitfully his Children about all 1'hings from the Mouth of the Lo1'(l; how he Mw, and heard and wrote them clown.]

And now, my children, I want you to understand that the Lord has revealed everything to me. My eyes have seen all things, from the very beginning to the end of time. I have written down everything I have witnessed in my books—the vast heavens, their endless space, and the countless beings that fill them. I have studied the paths of the stars and recorded their movements, even though their number is too great to count.

No human has ever seen the full course of the stars, and not even the angels know how many exist. Yet, I have written down each of their names. I have measured the path of the sun and the strength of its rays, tracking its rising and setting throughout every month of the year. I have carefully recorded all its movements and given them their proper names.

I have also studied the moon's orbit, tracking its daily phases and the hidden places it retreats to before rising again. I have followed its journey through time, measuring its path by the hours. I have defined the four seasons and divided them into four great cycles. Within these cycles, I arranged the years, set the months in order, and from the months, counted the days. From the days, I measured the hours.

Beyond the heavens, I have observed everything that moves upon the earth. I have recorded every living creature, every plant that is sown or grows naturally, and all vegetation found in gardens. Every herb, flower, and fragrance has been written down along with its name.

I have studied how clouds form and move, how they gather water and release rain. I have observed how raindrops fall and documented everything I have learned. I have tracked the paths of thunder and lightning, and I was shown the forces that control them. I saw the guardians who hold the keys to these powerful forces, releasing them in measured amounts so they do not destroy the earth.

I have recorded the storehouses of snow and hail and studied the gentle breezes. I saw the keeper of these elements, how he fills the clouds with snow and hail without ever running out. I observed the places where the winds rest and watched their keepers carefully measure and release them, ensuring they do not shake the earth with too much force.

I have measured the entire earth—its tallest mountains, rolling hills, vast fields, and thick forests. I have recorded the stones, rivers, and everything that exists on the land. I measured the height from the earth to the seventh heaven and the depths down to the lowest place of judgment. There, I saw the great abyss open, filled with cries of despair, where souls suffer as they await their final judgment.

I wrote down the names of those being judged, recording the punishments they received and the actions that led to their sentence. Every deed and its judgment have been documented in my writings, preserving the truth of what I have seen.

Chapter XL. 713

[How Enoch wept for the Sins of Adam.]

I saw all the people who came before us, starting with Adam and Eve, and I felt a deep sadness. Tears filled my eyes as I thought about the harm their mistakes had caused. Overwhelmed with sorrow, I cried out, "How unlucky I am, struggling with my own weaknesses and the failures of those before me!"

In my heart, I thought, "The luckiest people are the ones who were never born—or if they were, never did anything wrong against the Lord. They would never have to see this place or suffer its pain."

Chapters XLI. 1XLII. 6

I saw the gatekeepers of hell, standing tall like giant serpents. Their faces were dark and empty, like lamps that had gone out. Their fiery eyes burned fiercely, their sharp teeth shone, and they wore nothing on their upper bodies.

I stood before them and said, "I wish I had never seen you or heard of what you do. I wish no one from my family had ever come to this place. The people of my kind have made mistakes during their short time on earth, but now they must suffer forever."

From there, I traveled east to the paradise of Eden, a place of rest prepared for the good and righteous. It is connected to the third heaven but is hidden from this world. At its grand gates, where the sun rises, stand powerful angels surrounded by flames. They sing songs of victory, celebrating endlessly in the presence of the just.

On the final day, Adam and our ancestors will be brought into this paradise. They will enter with joy, like guests invited to a great feast. Together, they will arrive with happiness, share in cheerful conversations, and eagerly wait for the celebration—a feast filled with never-ending light, endless blessings, and a life of joy and laughter.

Then I said, "Listen to me, my children: Happy is the one who respects the Lord's name and serves Him with honesty. Blessed is the one who gives offerings with a sincere heart, who lives fairly, and who dies in righteousness.

Blessed is the one who judges fairly, not for rewards but because they love what is right. In the end, they will receive true justice. Blessed is the one who gives clothes to those in need and feeds the hungry. Blessed is the one who treats orphans and widows fairly and stands up for those who have been wronged.

Blessed is the one who turns away from the temporary and unstable things of this world and chooses the path of goodness, leading to eternal life. Blessed is the one who does good deeds, for they will receive even greater rewards.

Blessed is the one who speaks truthfully and has a kind and loving heart. Blessed is the one who understands the works of the Lord and gives Him praise. The Lord's ways are always right, and while people may do good or bad, each person is known by their actions."

Chapters XLII. 7—XLIII. 2

[Enoch shows his Children how he measured and wrote out the Judgements of God.]

Listen, my children, to the wisdom I have gathered in my life and the lessons I have reflected on from the Lord. I have written these thoughts down through the seasons, both in winter and summer. I have studied the passage of time, measured the years and hours, and carefully recorded their changes.

Just as one year can stand out more than another, people also differ from one another. Some are respected for their wealth, while others are honored for their wisdom. Some are known for their deep understanding, while others are admired for their clever thinking. A person might be valued for speaking softly, another for having a pure heart. Strength makes some stand out, while beauty makes others shine. Youth brings energy, while sharp thinking brings recognition. Some are praised for their sharp senses, while others are admired for their ability to understand and learn many things.

But let everyone remember this: no one is greater than the one who respects and follows God. That person will be the most honored and will remain strong and righteous forever.

Chapters XLIII. 3XLF. 4

[Enoch instructs his Sons that they should not revile the Person, of men, whether they are great or small.]

God created people with His own hands, shaping them in His own image. He made both the powerful and the weak, and anyone who mocks another person's appearance is insulting God Himself.

If someone becomes angry at another without a good reason, they will face the Lord's great anger. If a person spits on someone in disrespect, they will stand before God's judgment and face its consequences.

Blessed are those who hold no hatred in their hearts. Blessed are those who defend the mistreated, support the accused, lift up the oppressed, and answer the cries of those in need.

For on the day of judgment, every act of fairness—every scale, measurement, and tool of justice—will be tested and will receive its true reward.

Chapters XLVI. 1XLVIII. 1

[God shows that He does not wish Sacrifices from Man, nor Burnt Offerings, but pure and contrite Heart]

Whoever brings their offerings quickly before the Lord will also receive His blessings just as swiftly. God will ensure that justice is done for them. Whoever lights a lamp in His honor will find that their treasures in heaven grow even greater. But God does not actually need bread, light, animals, or any material gifts. These things have no real value to Him. What He truly desires is a heart that is honest and devoted. Through these offerings, He looks at what is inside a person's heart and tests their sincerity.

Think about how a king on earth would react if someone gave him a gift while secretly hiding bad intentions. If the king realized the person was being dishonest, wouldn't he reject the gift in anger and punish them? In the same way, if someone speaks kindly to another but secretly plans to hurt them, their deception will eventually be exposed, leading to shame. If people react this way, imagine how much more God despises and rejects gifts that come from dishonest hearts. He does not accept such offerings but instead turns away from them in anger.

One day, God will send a great light that will reveal everything. Both the good and the bad will be judged. No secret will remain hidden; every thought and intention will be exposed by His truth.

Now, my children, I urge you to keep these lessons close to your hearts. Think carefully about the words I have shared with you, for they do not come from me alone but from the Lord Himself. Hold on to these sacred teachings and study them carefully. In them, you will discover the incredible works of God. While many books have been written throughout history and more will continue to be written, none will reveal God's truth as clearly as these words.

If you follow these teachings and live by them, you will not turn away from God. Remember, there is no other God—nowhere in heaven, on earth, beneath the ground, or in the hidden depths of creation. Only He laid the unseen foundations of the world, stretched out the skies both visible and invisible, and set the earth upon the waters. He holds the waters in place without any solid ground beneath them, shaping everything in its endless beauty and variety.

Who but God can count every speck of dust on the earth, every grain of sand on the shore, every raindrop that falls, or each drop of morning dew? Who can measure the wind or control the land

and sea with unbreakable laws? Who shaped the stars from fire, decorated the sky, and placed the sun at its center, giving it light and warmth for all? Only the Lord, the Creator of everything, has done these things and more. His power has no limits, and His wisdom is beyond understanding.

Chapters XLVIII. 2XLIX.1

[Of the course of the Sun throughout the seven Circles.]

The sun moves through the seven layers of the sky, and I have given it 182 positions for the days when its path is shorter and 182 for when its path is longer. In addition, there are two special positions where it rests as it moves between its monthly cycles. Starting in the month of Tsivan, after seventeen days, the sun begins to move downward until the month of Thevan. Then, on the seventeenth day of Thevan, it begins to rise again.

This is how the sun follows its path in the sky. When it comes closer to the earth, the land is filled with joy, bringing an abundance of life and fruit. But when it moves farther away, the earth becomes dull, and trees and plants stop growing. Everything follows a precise and perfect order, set by God's endless wisdom, both in the visible world and beyond what we can see.

From the unseen, He created everything we see, though He Himself remains invisible. That is why, my children, I encourage you to share these writings with your families, your children, and people everywhere. Let those who are wise and respect God treasure these words. Let them value them more than the finest food, reading them with care and devotion.

But those who lack understanding and refuse to think about God will reject these teachings and turn away from them. For such people, judgment will come, and they will face the consequences.

Blessed is the one who accepts these teachings, carries them with faith, and follows them in life. That person will be free on the day of judgment and will stand in the light of truth and righteousness.

Chapters XLIX. 2LI. 2

[Enoch instructs his Sons not to swear either by the Heaven or the Earth; and shows the Promise of God to a Man even in the Womb of his Mother]

I tell you this, my children, with complete honesty. I will not swear by heaven, earth, or anything that God has made, because God Himself has said, "There is no swearing in Me, no injustice—only truth." If people do not have truth in their hearts, they should simply say "yes" when they mean yes and "no" when they mean no.

But I want you to know for certain—there has never been a single person born for whom a place has not already been prepared. Every soul has a purpose, and the time each person spends on this earth has already been set. So do not be misled, my children. Every soul has its own path and destination.

No one who has ever lived can hide from God, and nothing they do is truly secret. He sees everything, and I have written down the actions of every person. Each of us is given only a short time on earth, where we must face challenges and hardships. But during that time, we must never harm those who are vulnerable, like widows and orphans.

So, my children, live your days with patience and humility, and you will receive the gift of eternal life. Endure pain, hardships, and cruel words for the sake of the Lord. If someone wrongs you, do not seek revenge—not against a neighbor or even an enemy. Leave justice to God, for He alone will judge and repay when the time comes. Seeking revenge is not your place.

If any of you share your wealth to help a brother in need, you will be greatly rewarded on the day of judgment. Be generous to orphans, widows, and strangers, for acts of kindness are seen as treasures in the eyes of the Lord.

Chapters LI. 3LIII. 1

[Enoch instructs his Sons, not to hide their Treasures upon Earth, but lids them give Alms to the Needy.]

Help those in need as much as you can. Do not hide your wealth away—use it to support those who are honest but struggling. If you do, trouble will not come upon you when you face hardship. No matter what difficulties or challenges you must go through, endure them for the Lord's sake, and you will receive your reward on the day of judgment.

It is good to go to the house of the Lord in the morning, afternoon, and evening to honor the Creator of everything. Let all living things praise Him, and let every creature, seen and unseen, join in worship.

Blessed is the one who speaks to glorify the Lord and praises Him sincerely from the heart. But cursed is the one who uses their words to insult or harm others. Blessed is the one who lifts up God's name, but cursed is the one who spends their life speaking with anger, swearing, and showing disrespect.

Blessed is the one who appreciates and honors God's works, while cursed is the one who speaks badly about His creation. Blessed is the one who works hard and takes responsibility for their own efforts, but cursed is the one who relies on others without contributing. Blessed is the one who respects and upholds the traditions of their ancestors, while cursed is the one who disregards or destroys them.

Blessed is the one who brings peace and love among people. Cursed is the one who causes conflict and division. Blessed is the person who carries peace in their heart, not just talking about it but truly living it. However, cursed is the one who pretends to seek peace but secretly holds anger and resentment.

All these actions—both good and bad—are recorded, and on the day of judgment, everything will be revealed.

Chapters LIII. 2LVI. 1

[Let us not say that our Father is with God, and will plead for us at the Day of Judgment. For I know that a Father cannot help his Son, nor a Son a Father.]

Now, my children, do not think you can say, "Our father prays before God to free us from sin," because no one can take responsibility for another person's mistakes. Everyone is responsible for their own actions. I have recorded everything a person will do, even before they are born, just as it has been done for all people throughout time.

No one can change or erase what I have written, because God sees everything, even the hidden thoughts of those who do wrong. Nothing is truly secret from Him.

So, my children, listen carefully to my words. Do not ignore my advice only to regret it later and say, "Our father never warned us when we were lost in our foolishness." Pay attention now so that you do not look back with sadness, wishing you had known and done better.

Chapters LVI. 2LVIII. 5

[Enoch admonishes his Son that they should give the Books to Others.]

Let these books I am giving you be a gift of peace. Do not keep them hidden—share them with anyone who wants to learn. Encourage others to understand the incredible works of the Lord, which are beyond human understanding.

My children, my time with you is almost over. The moment is near when I must leave this world and go to heaven. Look, the angels are already here, waiting for God's command to take me. Tomorrow morning, I will go to the highest heavens, where I will live forever. So I urge you to do what is right in the eyes of the Lord and follow His ways.

Hearing this, Methuselah said to his father, "If it pleases you, Father, let me bring you food. Then, bless our homes, your sons, and our entire family so that your blessing may bring honor to your people. After that, you may go as God has commanded."

Enoch replied, "Listen, my son. Since the Lord anointed me with His glory, I no longer need earthly food. My soul has moved beyond the pleasures of this world, and I no longer desire anything from it."

Then Enoch said, "Call your brothers, their families, and the elders of the people so I may speak to them before I go, as the Lord has instructed me." Methuselah quickly gathered his brothers—Regim, Riman, Ukhan, Khermion, and Gaida—along with the elders of the people. They all came before Enoch, who blessed them and began to speak.

"My sons, listen to me. When the Lord first came to the earth for Adam's sake, He visited all of His creation. He gathered every animal, every creeping thing, and every bird in the sky and brought them before our father Adam. Adam named every living thing on earth, and the Lord made him ruler over all, placing everything under his care and commanding them to obey him. This is how God created man as the master of His creation.

But the Lord will not judge an animal because of a man's actions. Instead, He will judge people for how they have treated the animals. Just as there is a special place for every human soul, there is also a place for the souls of all creatures. Not a single soul that God has made will be lost before the great day of judgment. On that day, every animal will bear witness against the people who treated them unfairly, for the Lord sees everything and will judge with perfect justice."

Chapters LVIII. 6LIX. 4

[Enoch teaches all his Sons why they must not touch the Flesh of Cattle, because of what comes from it.]

Whoever treats animals cruelly or unfairly is also harming their own soul. When a person offers a clean animal as a sacrifice, they do so to protect their soul, recognizing that the life they take is meant for both nourishment and spiritual purpose. When done properly, this act is considered righteous and brings protection.

But if someone kills an animal carelessly or without respect, they hurt their own soul and commit a sin against themselves. It is a serious wrongdoing to harm any living creature without reason, as it reflects a heart filled with selfishness and cruelty. If a person secretly hurts an animal, it is an evil act that stains their soul, showing a lack of kindness and honesty.

Just as it is wrong to harm animals, it is even worse to harm another human—whether by physical harm or through wicked intentions. If someone causes suffering to another person's soul, they also bring suffering upon themselves, leaving no hope for forgiveness. Taking another person's life not only destroys them but also ruins the soul and body of the one who committed the act, cutting them off from redemption forever.

Anyone who sets a trap for another person will eventually fall into it themselves because deceit does not go unnoticed by God. A person who attacks their neighbor—whether with weapons or with harmful words—will have to face judgment and will not escape punishment. Speaking unfairly or acting unjustly toward someone else is a serious offense that takes away any claim to righteousness.

My children, guard your hearts against all forms of wrongdoing, for these are the things the Lord rejects. Just as you ask God for mercy, you should also show kindness and compassion to every living being. Let your actions reflect the goodness you hope to receive. Help those in need, especially the poor, and give generously from the work of your hands. In the world to come, nothing will be hidden—God sees everything, both good and bad. So live with fairness, kindness, and truth.

Chapters LIX. 5LXII. 1

There are many places prepared for people after this life, each one suited to their actions—good for those who lived righteously and bad for those who lived in evil. These places are endless in number, representing the eternal future of every person. Blessed are those who are worthy to enter the homes of the righteous, where they will live in peace and everlasting joy. But those who are sent to the homes of the wicked will find no rest, no relief, and no hope of escape.

Listen carefully, my children, both young and old. When a person thinks good thoughts and offers gifts to the Lord from their own hard work, their offering must come from what they have earned through honest effort. If someone presents a gift that they did not work for, the Lord will reject it, and it will bring them no benefit. Likewise, if someone works but complains in their heart and gives unwillingly, their gift will not be accepted, and they will gain nothing from it.

When offering gifts to the Lord, do so with faith and sincerity. Blessed is the person who brings their offering with patience, humility, and devotion, for this act can help atone for their sins. But do not waste time with empty talk or delay doing what must be done, for missing the right moment leads to loss. After death, there is no chance to make up for missed opportunities—what is lost on earth is lost forever. Doing things at the wrong time offends both people and God because it shows disrespect for His divine order.

When you see someone in need, do not look down on them. Instead, help them with kindness and a sincere heart. When a person gives clothing to the poor or feeds the hungry, they earn a reward from the Lord. But if they give while complaining or with a reluctant heart, they commit two wrongs—they take away the value of their gift and lose their own reward. Those who receive help must also be careful, for if a poor person takes what is given with pride or ungratefulness, they waste the lesson of their hardship and miss the chance to be blessed in return.

The Lord despises arrogance and lies. Every proud or hateful word, every dishonest act covered in deceit, is offensive to Him. Such wickedness is like a sharp sword that cuts through truth, and it will be thrown into the fire to burn forever. So, my children, live with humility, honesty, and faith, so that your actions will be pleasing to the Lord and bring you everlasting reward.

Chapters LXII. 2LXV.2

[How the Lord call8 Enoch: the People take Counsel to go to kiss him in the Place called Achuzan.]

When Enoch spoke these words to his sons and the elders, news of how the Lord had called him spread quickly. People from near and far heard about it and said to one another, "Let us go and see Enoch and honor him!"

Around two thousand people gathered at a place called Achuzan, where Enoch and his sons were staying. The elders and leaders of the people approached Enoch with great respect. They bowed before him, kissed him, and said, "Enoch, our father, may the Lord, the eternal King, bless you! Today, we ask that you bless your sons and all of us here so that we may be honored in your presence."

They continued, "You, Enoch, are forever glorified before the Lord. God has chosen you above all people on earth and made you the scribe of His creation, recording everything that is seen and unseen. You stand against the sins of men and protect your family."

Enoch listened to them and then spoke these words to his sons and to all who had gathered:

"Listen carefully, my children. Before anything existed, before any creature was made, the Lord created everything, both seen and unseen. When the right time came, He made man in His own image and likeness. He gave him eyes to see, ears to hear, a heart to understand, and the ability to think, make choices, and seek wisdom.

The Lord designed the world with mankind in mind. He created everything for man's sake, setting specific times for all things. From these times, He made years, from years He formed months, from months He shaped days, and from days He set seven in a cycle. Within these seven, He divided the hours into smaller parts so that man could understand the seasons and keep track of time—years, months, and hours. By knowing this, people could reflect on their lives from beginning to end, recognize their sins, and remember both their good and bad deeds.

For nothing is hidden from the Lord's sight. Each person must be aware of their actions and avoid breaking His commandments. Keep my writings safe and pass them down to future generations, for they contain wisdom and guidance for all.

When the time comes for all things, both visible and invisible, to reach their end—when the creation that the Lord Himself has made is completed—then all humanity will stand before Him in the great judgment. On that day, time itself will come to an end, and…"

Chapters LXV.2—LXVI.1

There will come a time when days, months, years, and hours will no longer exist. Time itself will stop being measured. Instead, there will be one eternal age where all those who have lived righteously and escaped God's great judgment will be gathered together to live forever. These good and faithful souls will exist in endless joy and unity, with no end to their happiness.

In this eternal life, there will be no hard work, no sickness, no sadness, no fear, no hunger, and no darkness. There will never be another night. A strong and unbreakable wall will surround them, keeping them safe. They will live in a bright and perfect paradise, where everything that can decay or be destroyed will be gone forever. This paradise will be their home forever, filled with the light of the Lord, free from pain and suffering.

As Enoch spoke to his sons and the elders, he reminded them to live with deep respect for God and to avoid anything that goes against His ways. He warned them to protect their souls from all forms of wrongdoing, for the Lord despises evil. "Serve only the Lord," he said. "Do not worship idols or anything made by human hands. Worship the Creator, who made the heavens, the earth, and everything in them. God is everywhere—in the skies, on the earth, and even in the deepest parts of the sea. Nothing is hidden from Him. He sees all that we do."

Enoch encouraged them to live with patience, humility, and love. He urged them to endure suffering, insults, and temptations, knowing that these struggles were temporary and that their reward would last forever. "Blessed are those who escape the great judgment," he said. "They will shine seven times brighter than the sun, for they have been set apart as righteous."

He reminded them of the order of creation—how God separated light from darkness, created paradise, and prepared the fires of judgment. He recorded all these things so they could read and understand them. His writings were meant to guide them, helping them stay faithful to God's commandments.

After Enoch finished speaking, a great darkness covered the land, like a heavy cloud surrounding the people. Suddenly, angels appeared and carried Enoch up to the highest heaven, where the Lord welcomed him into His presence. As Enoch rose, the darkness disappeared, and light returned to the earth. The people who witnessed this amazing event did not fully understand what had happened, but they praised God and went home, telling others what they had seen.

Enoch was born on the sixth day of the month of Tsivan, and he lived for 365 years. On the exact day and hour of his birth, he was taken up to heaven, completing his life on earth. Before leaving, Enoch spent thirty days writing about all of God's creations, producing 366 books. He left these writings with his sons as a lasting gift of divine wisdom.

After Enoch was taken to heaven, Methuselah and his brothers built an altar at Achuzan, the place where Enoch had ascended. They made sacrifices to the Lord and invited all the elders and people to join in a great celebration. The people brought gifts to Enoch's sons, and for three days, they rejoiced, praising God for the incredible sign He had shown through Enoch, a man who had received an extraordinary blessing from the Lord.

This celebration and the story of Enoch's life were passed down through generations as a reminder of God's greatness and mercy. It served as a lesson for all to remain faithful to the Lord, to love and serve Him, and to pass His commandments from one generation to the next. Amen.

Enoch III
The Hebrew Book of Enoch
(3 Enoch)

Chapter I

Rabbi Ishmael describes his journey into the heavens, where he saw the divine vision of the Merkaba, God's heavenly chariot. As he passed through each level, each one more incredible than the last, he finally reached the entrance to the seventh and highest realm. There, he stood in prayer before the Holy One, looking up at the brilliant light above. In his heart, he called upon the merit of Aaron, the son of Amram—a man known for spreading peace and kindness—who had been given the honor of priesthood directly by God on Mount Sinai.

Rabbi Ishmael prayed with deep emotion, asking that Aaron's righteousness protect him from Qafsiel, the ruling angel, and the other powerful beings guarding the entrance, so they would not harm him or stop him from entering. The Holy One heard his plea and sent Metatron, the Prince of the Presence, a great and exalted angel who serves closest to God's glory.

Metatron, shining with brilliant light, spread his wings in obedience and came down to meet Rabbi Ishmael. Taking his hand with strength yet gentleness, Metatron reassured him in the presence of the other heavenly beings, saying, "Come in peace before the great and mighty King, and behold the splendor of the Merkaba." With that, Rabbi Ishmael was led into the seventh Hall and brought before the dwelling place of the Divine Presence, where he stood before the Holy One and witnessed the incredible vision of the Merkaba.

The heavenly rulers of the Merkaba and the fiery Seraphim looked upon him, their radiant glow and piercing gaze overwhelming him with fear and awe. Their presence was so powerful that he trembled and collapsed, unable to withstand their brilliance. His strength faded as he was overcome by the splendor of their faces and the overwhelming glory surrounding him.

Seeing this, the Holy One rebuked the Seraphim, Kerubim, and Ophannim, saying, "My servants, my Seraphim, my Kerubim, and my Ophannim, turn your eyes away from Ishmael, my son, my friend, my beloved one, and my glory, so that he will not tremble in fear before you."

At God's command, Metatron, the ever-faithful Prince of the Presence, stepped forward and restored Rabbi Ishmael's spirit. He helped him stand, but even then, Rabbi Ishmael was too weak to speak a single word of praise before the Throne of Glory. The moment was too powerful, and he remained silent in awe. Only after an hour had passed did he finally regain the strength to lift his voice in worship.

Then, the Holy One opened the heavenly gates before him. But these were not ordinary gates—they were the gates of Divine Presence, Peace, Wisdom, Strength, Power, Speech, Song, Holiness, and Praise. As these sacred gates opened, Rabbi Ishmael's eyes were filled with light, and his heart overflowed with praise. He lifted his voice and sang psalms, songs, and praises, pouring out words of thanksgiving, glory, and worship.

As Rabbi Ishmael lifted his voice in a song of devotion and awe before the Holy One, the heavenly Chayyoth, both above and below the Throne of Glory, joined in perfect harmony. Their voices echoed with powerful cries of "HOLY" and "BLESSED BE THE GLORY OF YHWH FROM HIS PLACE!" Together, their praises rose high, filling the heavens as a tribute to the endless majesty and glory of the Divine King.

Chapter II

Rabbi Ishmael described an incredible moment when the highest angels—the mighty eagles of the Merkaba, the fiery Ophannim, and the blazing Seraphim—began to question his presence. Their voices, filled with authority and devotion to God, called out to Metatron, the exalted Prince of the Presence. Their words carried both curiosity and amazement.

"Young one," they said, addressing Metatron with a title that reflected his strength and closeness to God. "Why do you allow a human, someone born on earth, to enter this holy place and witness the sacred vision of the Merkaba? Where is he from? What tribe does he belong to? What makes him worthy of such an honor?"

Metatron, always faithful to his role, answered with respect and confidence. "He is from the nation of Israel, the people chosen by the Holy One out of all seventy nations. This nation was set apart to carry His name and follow His commandments. He comes from the tribe of Levi, the tribe dedicated to God's service. He is a descendant of Aaron, whom the Holy One Himself chose and honored with the crown of priesthood at Mount Sinai."

When the angels heard this, they accepted his answer. Their awe turned into recognition, and they understood the privilege that had been given to Rabbi Ishmael. Their voices, now filled with praise, spoke of the holiness of Israel.

"Indeed," they said, "this man is worthy to see the Merkaba. Blessed is the nation that has him among their people."

Their words of joy and reverence echoed through the heavenly realms as they declared, "Happy is the people who are given such a blessing!" Their proclamation was not just about Rabbi Ishmael's honor—it was a reminder of the special connection between God and His people, a bond that sets apart those chosen to serve Him.

Chapter III

Metatron has seventy names, but God calls him "Youth."

Rabbi Ishmael said:

At that moment, I asked Metatron, the angel and Prince of the Presence, "What is your name?"

He answered, "I have seventy names, each one tied to the seventy languages of the world. But all of them are connected to my main name, Metatron, the angel of the Presence. However, my King calls me 'Youth' (Na'ar)."

Chapter IV

Metatron is the same as Enoch, who was taken to heaven before the Great Flood.

Rabbi Ishmael said:

I asked Metatron, "Why do you share a name with the Creator and have seventy different names? You are greater than all the heavenly rulers, higher than all the angels, and more beloved than any of God's servants. You have more power, authority, and glory than all the mighty ones. So why, in the highest heavens, are you still called 'Youth'?"

He answered, "I am Enoch, the son of Jared. When the people of the Flood turned away from God and lived in corruption, they rejected Him, saying, 'Leave us alone; we want nothing to do with Your ways' (Job 21:14). At that time, the Holy One took me from the world. He brought me to the heavens so that I could serve as a witness against them for all future generations. This way, no one could ever claim that God was unjust.

But why was everyone destroyed? What had their wives, children, or animals done? Why were their horses, mules, cattle, and all their possessions—even the birds—wiped out by the Flood? If the people had sinned, what wrong did the children commit? What could the animals and birds have done to deserve such destruction? How could anyone say it was fair that the innocent were punished along with the wicked?

Because of these questions, the Holy One took me up while the people were still alive, allowing them to witness my ascension. He made me a testimony to His justice. He then appointed me as a prince and leader among the ministering angels.

At that moment, three powerful angels—Uzza, Azza, and Azazel—stepped forward and accused me before the Holy One. They said, "Didn't the First Ones—the ancient angels—warn You not to create humans?"

The Holy One replied, "I created them, and I will take care of them. I will carry them, and I will save them" (Isaiah 46:4).

When the angels saw me, they protested, "Lord of the Universe! Why is this human allowed to rise to the heavens? Is he not a descendant of those who were destroyed in the Flood? Why has he been brought here?"

The Holy One responded, "Who are you to question Me? I find more joy in this one than in all of you. Therefore, he will be a prince and a ruler over you in the high heavens."

Immediately, the angels accepted God's decision. They came to me, bowed, and said, "Blessed are you, and blessed is your father, for your Creator has given you great honor."

And because I am still young compared to them in days, months, and years, they call me 'Youth' (Na'ar)."

Chapter V

The idolatry of Enosh's generation caused God to remove His presence from the earth.

Rabbi Ishmael said:

Metatron, the Prince of the Presence, explained to me:

From the day that the Holy One removed Adam from the Garden of Eden, His presence, the Shekina, remained on a Kerub beneath the Tree of Life. During that time, angels would descend from heaven in organized groups, traveling through the skies in great numbers to carry out His will across the world.

Adam and his descendants stood outside the gates of the Garden, gazing in awe at the brilliant light of the Shekina. Its radiance spread across the entire world, shining 3,000 times brighter than the sun. Anyone who stood in its light lived without suffering—there were no flies, no gnats, no sickness, no pain, and no harm from demons.

Whenever the Holy One moved—from the Garden to Eden, from Eden back to the Garden, then to the sky, and back again— His presence remained visible to all without causing harm. This divine light stayed on earth until the time of Enosh's generation, when people turned away from God and began worshiping idols.

What did the people of Enosh's time do? They traveled across the earth, gathering silver, gold, gems, and pearls. They built massive piles of treasure and used them to carve gigantic idols, each one as large as 1,000 parasangs. Around these idols, they placed the sun, moon, stars, and planets, believing these celestial forces would serve their idols just as they served the Holy One. Their actions reflected what is written in 1 Kings 22:19: "And all the host of heaven was standing by Him on His right hand and on His left."

But how did they accomplish such a thing? They could not have done this without the help of the fallen angels Azza, Uzza, and Azziel, who taught them the forbidden secrets of magic. Using these dark arts, they learned to control and manipulate heavenly forces to serve their idols.

At that time, the angels who served the Holy One brought their concerns before Him, saying, "Master of the World, why do You still care for humans? As it is written in Psalms 8:4, 'What is man (Enosh) that You are mindful of him?' It does not say 'What is Adam,' but 'What is Enosh,' for he has become the leader of idol worshippers.

Why have You left the highest heavens—the glorious realm where Your exalted Name is praised, the place of Your majestic and elevated Throne in Araboth? The heavens of Araboth, the highest of the heavens, are filled with Your splendor, might, and greatness. Your Throne there is lifted above all things.

And yet, You have come down to live among the children of men, who worship idols and compare You to their false gods. Now, You are on earth, but so are their lifeless idols. Why do You remain among people who have turned their backs on You?"

Immediately, the Holy One removed His Shekina from the earth and withdrew His presence from among them.

At that moment, the angels of heaven, along with the hosts and armies of Araboth—countless in number—gathered around the Shekina. They held trumpets and horns in their hands, forming a great procession as they lifted their voices in songs of praise. Surrounded by their music and worship, the Shekina rose to the highest heavens, just as it is written in Psalms 47:3:

"God has gone up with a shout, the Lord with the sound of a trumpet."

Chapter VI

Enoch Ascends to Heaven with the Shekina, and the Angels Question God

Rabbi Ishmael said:

Metatron, the Angel and Prince of the Presence, explained to me:

When the Holy One decided to bring me up to heaven, He first sent Metatron to carry out His command. In front of everyone around me, Metatron appeared and took me away. He carried me in a brilliant blaze of fire, riding on a chariot of flames pulled by fiery horses—servants of divine glory. Surrounded by a glowing light, I rose up and ascended together with the Shekina to the highest heavens.

As soon as I arrived, the holy angels—Chayyoth, Ophannim, Seraphim, Kerubim, and the Wheels of the Merkaba (the Galgallim)—along with the ministers of the fiery presence, became aware of me. They sensed my approach from an incredible distance—36,000 myriads of parasangs away. Smelling my essence, they were astonished and cried out in disbelief:

"What is this scent of a human? What is this trace of a mortal, formed from a tiny drop of flesh, daring to rise to the highest heavens? How can someone born of the earth enter this place and stand among those who are made of fire?"

Still amazed, they continued, saying:

"How can a being of flesh and blood reach this realm? How can a human, created from dust, stand among those who dwell in divine fire?"

Hearing their protests, the Holy One answered them:

"My servants, my heavenly hosts—my Kerubim, my Ophannim, my Seraphim—do not be troubled or upset by this! Listen carefully and understand. Nearly all the people on earth have turned away from Me. They have rejected My kingdom, abandoned My ways, and chosen to worship idols and false gods. Because of their actions, I have removed My Shekina from the earth and lifted it up to the heavens, far from them.

But this one is different. He is special, chosen, and precious among all who live on earth. He is unique, set apart by his faith, unwavering in righteousness, and pure in his actions. His devotion is greater than anyone else's, and he is worthy of this honor. I have taken him from the world as an offering—a soul of great value, chosen from all beneath the heavens to serve in My presence."

Chapter VII

Enoch Is Lifted to the Throne, the Merkaba, and the Angelic Hosts

Rabbi Ishmael said:

Metatron, the Angel and Prince of the Presence, explained to me:

When the Holy One decided to take me away from the generation of the Flood, He lifted me up on the wings of the Shekina's divine wind. Carried by this sacred force, I rose to the highest heavens, beyond anything that can be understood on earth. He brought me into the magnificent palaces of Araboth Raqia', a realm of incredible beauty and greatness.

There, I saw the glorious Throne of the Shekina, shining with a brilliance beyond words. Around it stood the great Merkaba, the divine chariot, surrounded by countless heavenly beings. I saw the troops of anger, fierce in their power, and the armies of judgment, ready to carry out God's will. Encircling the Throne were the fiery

Shin'nim, beings of intense light, and the blazing Kerubim, whose radiance was beyond understanding.

The burning Ophannim, wheels of divine fire, moved with endless energy, while the flashing Chashmallim sent out waves of glowing light and mystery. The Seraphim, creatures of pure lightning and flame, hovered nearby, their presence both overwhelming and humbling.

In the middle of this vast, heavenly assembly, the Holy One gave me a special and sacred role. He placed me before the Throne of Glory to serve and stand in His presence every day, witnessing the greatness and beauty that fill the highest heavens.

Chapter VIII

The gates of the treasuries of heaven opened to Metatron

Rabbi Ishmael said:

Metatron, the Prince of the Presence, told me:

Before the Holy One appointed me to serve at the Throne of Glory, He opened for me three hundred thousand gates of wisdom, understanding, kindness, love, humility, mercy, Torah, and reverence for heaven. Each gate unlocked a deeper level of knowledge and virtue, preparing me for my role.

At that moment, the Holy One increased my wisdom, adding layer upon layer of understanding. He deepened my awareness, sharpening my ability to see the finest details of divine truth. He filled me with knowledge upon knowledge, expanding my ability to comprehend His ways. He poured mercy upon mercy into me, strengthening my compassion for all creation. He gave me instruction upon instruction, enhancing my ability to teach and guide with absolute clarity.

He multiplied my love, making my heart overflow with kindness, and filled me with goodness upon goodness, creating an endless well of virtue within me. He clothed me in humility upon humility, grounding my spirit in true meekness. He strengthened me with power upon power, increasing my abilities beyond understanding. He gave me might upon might, allowing me to stand firm and unwavering in my tasks. He filled me with light upon light, making my brilliance shine even brighter than before.

He enhanced my beauty, increasing it until I reflected the splendor of His presence. He covered me in glory upon glory, making me shine with the radiance of His greatness. With all these gifts, I was honored and blessed, receiving qualities greater than any of the children of heaven. He elevated me above them all, granting me virtues and wisdom beyond what any other heavenly being had ever received.

Chapter IX

Enoch Is Blessed and Transformed with Angelic Features

Rabbi Ishmael said:

Metatron, the Prince of the Presence, explained to me:

After everything that had happened, the Holy One placed His hand upon me and gave me fifty-three unique blessings.

He then lifted me up and expanded my size until I stretched across the entire world, both in length and width.

He caused twenty-two wings to grow on me, with thirty-six wings on each side. Each wing was as vast as the whole world itself.

He gave me three hundred sixty-three eyes, and each one shined as brightly as the great light in the heavens.

He adorned me with unmatched splendor, brilliance, radiance, and beauty, filling me with the light of the entire universe. There was no form of majesty or glory that He did not place upon me.

Chapter X

God placed Metatron on a throne at the entrance of the highest hall and sent a messenger to announce his new role. Metatron was now God's representative, ruling over all the heavenly beings and the leaders of different realms—except for eight powerful princes who carried the sacred name of their King.

Rabbi Ishmael said: Metatron, the Prince of the Presence, explained to me:

"The Holy One, blessed be He, did all of this for me. He created a special throne for me, designed to look like the glorious Throne of God. He covered it with a curtain full of light, beauty, kindness, and mercy, shining just like the one before God's own throne. This curtain was decorated with all the lights of the universe, glowing in their full brilliance.

He placed this throne at the entrance of the Seventh Hall and seated me upon it. Then a messenger traveled through the heavens, declaring:

'This is Metatron, my servant. I have made him a prince and a ruler over all the leaders of my kingdoms and the heavenly beings—except for the eight great princes who bear the sacred name of their King.

From now on, any angel or prince who wishes to bring a matter before me must first go to him. They will speak to him, and he will represent them before me. Whatever command he gives in my name must be followed.

I have placed him under the care of the Prince of Wisdom and the Prince of Understanding, who will teach him the mysteries of heaven and earth, as well as the knowledge of this world and the next.

I have also put him in charge of all the treasuries in the heavenly palaces and all the stores of life that I possess in the highest heavens."'

Chapter XI

God reveals all hidden knowledge to Metatron.

Rabbi Ishmael said: Metatron, the angel and Prince of the Presence, explained to me:

"From that moment on, the Holy One, blessed be He, showed me every mystery of the Torah and all the deepest secrets of wisdom. He let me understand the true depths of the Law, the thoughts of every living being, and the hidden truths of the universe. Every secret of Creation was made clear to me, just as they are fully known to the Creator Himself.

I carefully observed the mysteries of the universe and the wonders hidden within them. Before anyone even had a secret thought, I already knew it. Before something was created, I had already seen it.

There was nothing in the heavens above or in the depths below that was beyond my knowledge. Even before a person formed an idea, I understood their thoughts. Nothing in the highest places or the lowest depths was hidden from me."

Chapter XII

God gives Metatron a robe of glory, crowns him, and calls him "the Lesser VHWH."

Rabbi Ishmael said: Metatron, the Prince of the Presence, explained to me:

"Because of the deep love the Holy One, blessed be He, had for me—more than for any of the other heavenly beings—He made me a special garment of glory. This robe was covered in dazzling light, and He dressed me in it.

He also created a second robe for me, one of honor, decorated with beauty, brilliance, and majesty. Then, He placed it on me as well.

After that, He made a royal crown just for me. It was set with forty-nine precious stones, each glowing as brightly as the sun.

The light from this crown shone in every direction, spreading across the highest heavens, through all seven levels, and to the farthest corners of the world. Then, He placed it upon my head.

Finally, in front of all the heavenly beings, He called me 'The Lesser VHWH,' as it is written in Exodus 23:21: 'For My Name is in him.'"

Chapter XIII

God writes the letters of creation on Metatron's crown with a flaming pen.

Rabbi Ishmael said: Metatron, the angel and Prince of the Presence, explained to me:

"Because of the great love and kindness the Holy One, blessed be He, had for me—more than for any other heavenly being—He used His own finger to write on the crown placed upon my head. With a pen of fire, He engraved the sacred letters by which the heavens and the earth were created.

These same letters brought the seas, rivers, mountains, and hills into existence. They shaped the planets, stars, and all the forces of nature. The winds, lightning, earthquakes, and thunder came from them, as did snow, hail, and storms. Every element of the world and the entire structure of Creation was formed by these letters.

Each letter on my crown glowed with an unending light. At times, they flashed like lightning. Other times, they burned like torches or flickered like flames. Their brightness was as powerful as the sun, the moon, and the stars, shining across the heavens.

When the Holy One, blessed be He, placed this crown upon my head, all the rulers of the heavenly realms trembled before me. The highest princes and the strongest angels—those greater than all the others who stand before God's Throne—shook with fear.

Even Sammael, the Prince of the Accusers, the mightiest of all the rulers of the heavens, was filled with dread when he saw me.

The angels who govern the forces of nature—the angel of fire, the angel of hail, the angel of wind, the angel of lightning, the angel of wrath, the angel of thunder, the angel of snow, the angel of rain, the angel of the day, the angel of the night, the angel of the sun, the angel of the moon, the angel of the planets, and the angel of the stars—all of them, powerful in their own right, trembled at the sight of me.

These rulers of the world have names:

- Gabriel, ruler of fire
- Baradiel, ruler of hail
- Ruchiel, ruler of the wind
- Baragiel, ruler of lightning
- Za'amiel, ruler of wrath
- Ziqiel, ruler of sparks
- Zi'iel, ruler of disturbances
- Za'aphiel, ruler of storms
- Ra'amiel, ruler of thunder
- Ra'ashiel, ruler of earthquakes
- Shafgiel, ruler of snow

- Matariel, ruler of rain
- Shimshiel, ruler of the day
- Lailiel, ruler of the night
- Galgalliel, ruler of the sun
- 'Ophanniel, ruler of the moon
- Kohbiel, ruler of the planets
- Rahatiel, ruler of the stars

When all these powerful beings saw me, they fell to the ground, unable to look at me. The dazzling light that shone from the crown on my head was so overwhelming that they were struck with awe, unable to lift their eyes to meet mine."

Chapter XIV

Metatron Transformed into Fire

Rabbi Ishmael said: Metatron, the angel and Prince of the Presence, explained to me:

"When the Holy One, blessed be He, chose me to serve at His Throne of Glory, to assist with the divine chariot and the presence of His majesty, my very being was transformed. My body turned into flames of fire, my muscles became blazing sparks, and my bones glowed like burning coals. The light from my eyelids flashed like lightning, my eyes burned like fiery embers, and my hair became flames. Every part of me turned into wings of fire, and my whole form radiated with intense heat.

On my right, streams of fire flowed endlessly, and on my left, burning flames erupted. Stormwinds and tempests surrounded me, while the sound of roaring thunder and shaking earth echoed before and behind me."

Rabbi Ishmael said: Metatron, the highest of all princes, stands before the One greater than all other powers. He moves beneath the Throne of Glory and dwells in a magnificent home of light above. From there, he gathers the fire of deafness and places it into the ears of the heavenly creatures, so they cannot hear the overwhelming voice of God's word.

When Moses climbed to the heights, he fasted for forty days and nights until the secret places of divine energy were revealed to him. He saw the purest, deepest heart within the heart of the Lion, shining as white as its very core. Around him stood countless angels, their presence filled with blazing fire, and they longed to consume him. But Moses prayed—first for the people of Israel and then for himself.

The One who sits upon the divine chariot opened the windows above the cherubim. A vast group of 1,800 angelic beings, along with Metatron, the Prince of the Presence, came out to meet Moses. They gathered the prayers of Israel, shaped them into a crown, and placed it upon the head of the Holy One, blessed be He.

Then they proclaimed, "Hear, O Israel: the Lord our God, the Lord is One." Their faces shone with joy, and the Divine Presence radiated with brilliant light. The Shekina rejoiced, and the angels asked Metatron, "What is this great honor? Who is it for?" The answer came: "It is for the Glorious Lord of Israel."

They declared again, "Hear, O Israel: the Lord our God is One, the Eternal King who lives forever."

At that moment, Akatriel Yah Yehod Sebaoth spoke to Metatron and commanded, "Let no prayer from Moses go unanswered. Listen to his requests and grant them, no matter how big or small."

Then Metatron turned to Moses and said, "Son of Amram, do not be afraid. God is pleased with you! Ask for whatever you desire from His Glory. Your face shines with a light that stretches across the world."

But Moses hesitated. "I fear that I might bring guilt upon myself," he said.

Metatron reassured him, "Take hold of the sacred letters of the oath. They are unbreakable and guarantee that the covenant will never be broken."

Chapter XV

Metatron Divested of His Privilege of Presiding on a Throne of His Own on Account of Acher's Misunderstanding, Thinking Him a Second Divine Power

Rabbi Ishmael said: Metatron, the angel and Prince of the Presence, explained to me:

"At first, I sat on a great throne at the entrance of the Seventh Hall. From there, I carried out judgments for the heavenly beings, ruling over the divine hosts under the authority of the Holy One, blessed be He. I was given the power to grant greatness, kingship, honor, rulership, and glory to the princes of the heavenly realms. While overseeing the Celestial Court, I remained seated, while the princes of the kingdoms stood before me—some to my right and others to my left—all by the command of the Holy One.

But when Acher entered and saw the vision of the divine chariot, he became overwhelmed with fear. His soul trembled, and he nearly lost himself, overcome by terror and awe. He saw me seated on a throne like a king, with countless angels standing around me as attendants. The crowned rulers of the heavens stood in my presence, and the sight filled him with confusion and dread.

In his shock, he spoke aloud and said, 'Surely, there must be two divine powers in heaven!'

Immediately, a divine voice rang out from heaven, from the presence of the Shekina, declaring: 'Return, O wayward children—except for Acher!'

Then Aniyel, a mighty and honored prince, a being of great majesty and power, was sent on a mission from the Holy One, blessed be He. He struck me sixty times with lashes of fire and commanded me to rise to my feet."

Chapter XVI

The Princes of the Seven Heavens, of the Sun, Moon, Planets, and Constellations and Their Hosts of Angels

Rabbi Ishmael said: Metatron, the angel and Prince of the Presence, explained to me:

"There are seven great princes, each of them magnificent, respected, and full of wonder. They have been placed in charge of the seven heavens. Their names are Mikael, Gabriel, Shatqiel, Shachaqiel, Bakariel, Badariel, and Pachriel.

Each of these princes rules over a different heaven and leads a vast host of 496,000 groups of ministering angels.

- Mikael, the highest prince, governs the seventh and highest heaven, Araboth.
- Gabriel, leader of the heavenly armies, rules over the sixth heaven, Maban.
- Shatqiel, another powerful prince, is in charge of the fifth heaven, Ma'an.
- Shachaqiel oversees the fourth heaven, Ja'uf.
- Badariel commands the third heaven, Shejaqim.
- Barakiel rules over the second heaven, Raqia'.
- Pachriel governs the first heaven, Wilan, which is within Shamayim.

Below them is Algalliel, the prince responsible for the movement of the sun. He is accompanied by 96 great and honored angels who guide the sun's path through the heavens of Raqia'.

Beneath them is Ophanniel, the prince who controls the moon's journey. With him are 84 angels who move the moon along its orbit. Each night, they guide it 354,000 parasangs, especially on the fifteenth day of the month when it reaches its turning point in the East.

Next is Rahatiel, the prince in charge of the stars and constellations. He is assisted by seven great and powerful angels. His name, Rahatiel, comes from his task—guiding the stars as they move through the sky. Each night, he leads them 339,000 parasangs, moving them from East to West and back again. The Holy One, blessed be He, has created a special path for them—a place where the sun, moon, planets, and stars rest as they travel from West to East during the night.

Following him is Kokbiel, the prince who rules over the planets. With him are 354,000 groups of ministering angels. These powerful angels guide the planets, moving them from one city and province to another within the heavens of Raqia'.

Above them all are seventy-two princes of the heavenly kingdoms, each corresponding to one of the seventy languages spoken on Earth. These princes wear royal crowns, are dressed in robes of honor, and are wrapped in magnificent cloaks. They ride royal horses and carry scepters, displaying their great authority.

As they travel through the heavens, servants run ahead of them, announcing their arrival with grand celebration. Just as earthly rulers travel with chariots, horsemen, and great armies, so do these heavenly princes make their way through Raqia'. Their journeys are marked with majesty, splendor, songs of praise, and honor. Vast armies of angels accompany them, singing and rejoicing in their greatness, just as people do when earthly kings travel in magnificent processions."

Chapter XVII

The order of ranks of the angels and the homage received by the higher ranks from the lower ones

Rabbi Ishmael said: Metatron, the angel and Prince of the Presence, explained to me:

"The angels of the first heaven, whenever they see their prince, immediately get off their heavenly horses and bow down, pressing their faces to the ground in respect. The prince of the first heaven, when he sees the prince of the second heaven, also dismounts, removes his crown, and falls on his face in humility.

The prince of the second heaven, upon seeing the prince of the third heaven, takes off his crown and bows down in awe. Likewise, the prince of the third heaven, when he sees the prince of the fourth heaven, removes his crown and lowers himself to the ground in deep respect.

The prince of the fourth heaven, when he meets the prince of the fifth heaven, does the same—removing his crown and bowing with his face to the ground. The prince of the fifth heaven, upon seeing the prince of the sixth heaven, also removes his crown and falls on his face in reverence.

The prince of the sixth heaven, when he sees the prince of the seventh heaven, takes off his crown and bows, trembling with awe. The prince of the seventh heaven, upon meeting the seventy-two princes of the heavenly kingdoms, removes his crown and falls on his face in deep humility.

The seventy-two princes, when they approach the gatekeepers of the first hall in the highest heaven, Araboth Raqia', remove their crowns and bow low in honor.

The gatekeepers of the first hall, when they see the gatekeepers of the second hall, also take off their crowns and lower themselves to the ground. The gatekeepers of the second hall, upon meeting those of the third hall, do the same—removing their crowns and bowing in respect.

This continues at every level:

- The gatekeepers of the third hall bow before those of the fourth hall.
- The fourth hall's gatekeepers bow before those of the fifth.
- The fifth hall's gatekeepers lower themselves before the sixth.
- The sixth hall's gatekeepers fall on their faces before those of the seventh.

When the gatekeepers of the seventh hall see the four great princes—the most honored ones, appointed over the four camps of the Divine Presence—they take off their crowns and bow in complete submission.

The four great princes, when they see the highest prince—the one who leads all of heaven in song and praise—remove their crowns and lower their faces to the ground in worship.

Tag'as, the great and honored prince, when he encounters Barattiel, the mighty prince who stands three fingers high in the highest heaven, Araboth, removes his crown and bows deeply to the ground.

Barattiel, when he sees Hamon, the powerful and revered prince, who is both awe-inspiring and magnificent—so powerful that all of heaven trembles when he calls out the 'Thrice Holy'—removes his crown and falls on his face in fear and respect.

Hamon, when he meets Tutresiel, another mighty prince, takes off his crown and bows to the ground. Tutresiel, when he sees Atrugiel, the great prince, also removes his crown and lowers his face in deep reverence."

Atrugiel, the great prince, when he sees Na'aririel, another great prince, removes his crown and bows down with his face to the ground.

Na'aririel, when he meets Sasnigiel, takes off his crown and lowers himself in respect. Sasnigiel, upon seeing Zazriel, removes his crown and bows deeply to show honor. Zazriel, when he encounters Geburatiel, does the same—taking off his crown and falling on his face in humility.

Geburatiel, when he sees 'Anaphiel, removes his crown and bows low. 'Anaphiel, when he meets Ashruylu, the prince who oversees all heavenly gatherings, also removes his crown and lowers himself in submission.

Ashruylu, when he sees Callisur, the prince who reveals the secrets of the divine law, takes off his crown and bows with his face to the ground in reverence. Callisur, when he meets Zakzakiel, the prince responsible for recording Israel's deeds before the Throne of Glory, removes his crown and falls on his face in humility.

Zakzakiel, upon seeing 'Anaphiel, the prince who holds the keys to the heavenly halls, also removes his crown and bows low. Why is he called 'Anaphiel? Because his honor, brilliance, and majestic presence spread throughout all the heavenly chambers, much like the Creator's glory fills the universe, as written in Habakkuk 3:3: "His glory covered the heavens, and the earth was full of His praise." In the same way, 'Anaphiel's greatness overshadows all the splendor of Araboth, the highest heaven.

When 'Anaphiel sees Sother Ashiel, a mighty and revered prince, he removes his crown and lowers himself in awe. Why is he called Sother Ashiel? Because he is in charge of the four streams of the fiery river that flows before the Throne of Glory. Every heavenly being must have his permission to enter or leave the presence of the Divine. He controls the seals of the fiery river, and his towering height measures 7,000 myriads of parasangs. When he moves before the Divine Presence, he stirs the flames of the river and declares what is written about the deeds of the world, as described in Daniel 7:10: "The judgment was set, and the books were opened."

Sother Ashiel, when he sees Shoqed Chozi, a powerful and fearsome prince, removes his crown and bows low. Why is Shoqed Chozi given this name? Because he weighs all human actions on a balance before the Holy One, blessed be He.

When Shoqed Chozi sees Zehanpuryu, a mighty and honored prince feared by all the heavenly hosts, he takes off his crown and bows in humility. Why is Zehanpuryu called by this name? Because he has the power to command the fiery river and send it back to its source.

When Zehanpuryu sees Azbuga, a prince greatly revered and exalted among those who understand the mysteries of the Throne of Glory, he removes his crown and bows down in awe. Why is Azbuga called by this name? Because in the future, he will clothe the righteous in garments of life and wrap them in robes of light, preparing them for eternal life.

When Azbuga sees two great and powerful princes standing above him, he removes his crown and falls to the ground in deep respect. These two princes are known as Sopheriel H' the Killer and Sopheriel H' the Lifegiver. Both are ancient, mighty, and beyond reproach.

Why is one called Sopheriel H' the Killer? Because he is responsible for the book of the dead, recording the names of those whose time has come. Why is the other called Sopheriel H' the Lifegiver? Because he oversees the book of life, where the names of those whom God grants life are written, according to His will.

You may wonder, "Since God sits on a throne, do these princes also sit while writing?" The Scriptures teach (1 Kings 22:19, 2 Chronicles 18:18): "And all the host of heaven stands by Him." This makes it clear that even the greatest heavenly beings perform their duties while standing.

But how do they write while standing? One stands on the wheels of a storm, and the other stands on the wheels of a whirlwind. They wear royal garments and are wrapped in majestic cloaks. Both wear crowns of glory. Their entire bodies are covered in eyes, and they shine as brightly as lightning. Their eyes glow like the sun at full strength, and their height stretches across all seven heavens. Their wings are as numerous as the days of the year and spread across the entire expanse of the sky.

Their lips are as wide as the gates of the East, and their tongues rise as high as the waves of the ocean. Flames pour from their mouths, and their tongues burn like torches. A sapphire stone rests on each of their heads, and on their shoulders are wheels driven by swift cherubim. One holds a fiery scroll, while the other holds a flaming pen. The scroll is 30,000 myriads of parasangs long, the pen measures 3,000 myriads, and each letter they write is 365 parasangs in size.

Chapter XVIII

Ribbiel, the Prince of the Wheels of the Merkaba, and the Surroundings of the Merkaba. The Commotion Among the Angelic Hosts During the Qedushsha

Rabbi Ishmael said: Metatron, the angel and Prince of the Presence, explained to me:

"Above these three powerful angels, there is one prince who stands apart from all others. He is honored, noble, and glorious, feared for his strength and might. He is magnificent, crowned with greatness, exalted, and beloved. There is no other prince like him. His name is Ribbiel, the great and revered prince who stands by the divine chariot.

Why is he called Ribbiel? Because he has been given authority over the wheels of the divine chariot, and they are under his control.

How many wheels are there? There are eight in total—two in each direction. Around them are four powerful winds, each with its own name: Storm Wind, Tempest, Strong Wind, and Wind of Earthquake.

Beneath the wheels, four fiery rivers flow, one on each side. Between these rivers stand four massive clouds. These clouds are known as clouds of fire, clouds of lamps, clouds of coal, and clouds of brimstone. Positioned around the wheels, they create a scene of overwhelming power and energy.

The feet of the heavenly creatures rest upon these wheels. Between each wheel, the sound of roaring earthquakes and crashing thunder echoes through the heavens.

When the moment comes for the great Song to be sung, the wheels begin to move, and the clouds shake.

At that time, all of heaven trembles:

- The mighty leaders become afraid.
- The horsemen grow restless.
- The warriors are shaken.
- The heavenly armies are filled with fear.
- The ranks of angels are overwhelmed.
- The appointed ones rush away in alarm.
- The commanders and soldiers are filled with dread.
- The servants grow weak.
- Every angel and heavenly division trembles in awe.

As the wheels turn, they call out to one another. One crown speaks to another, one heavenly creature calls to the next, and one Seraph reaches out to another, saying, as it is written in Psalm 68:3:

'Praise Him who rides upon the heavens, by His name Yah, and rejoice before Him!'"

Chapter XIX

Rabbi Ishmael said: Metatron, the angel and Prince of the Presence, explained to me:

"Above all these stands one great and powerful prince. His name is Chayy'liel. He is noble and honored, full of strength and glory. He is so mighty that all the heavenly beings tremble before him. His power is so great that he could swallow the entire earth in a single moment, as if with one bite.

Why is he called Chayy'liel? Because he has been placed in charge of the Holy Chayyoth. He strikes them with lashes of fire to stir them into action, and when they sing praises, he honors them. He urges them to proclaim, 'Holy, holy, holy,' and 'Blessed be the glory of the Lord from His place!' during the great hymn of praise."

Chapter XX

The Chayyoth

Rabbi Ishmael said: Metatron, the angel and Prince of the Presence, explained to me:

"There are four great heavenly beings, called the Chayyoth, each connected to one of the four winds. Every one of them is as vast as the entire world. Each has four faces, and all their faces look toward the East.

Each Chayyâ has four enormous wings, each as large as the roof of the universe. Their faces contain even more faces within them, and their wings have layers upon layers of wings. The size of their faces is equal to 248 faces, and their wings are as massive as 363 wings combined.

Each of these beings wears 2,000 crowns on its head. Every crown is as beautiful as a rainbow in the sky and shines as brightly as the sun. Sparks of light radiate from them, glowing like the morning star, the planet Venus, as it rises in the East."

Chapter XXI (A)

Kerubiel, the Prince of the Kerubim, and the Description of the Kerubim

Rabbi Ishmael said: Metatron, the angel and Prince of the Presence, explained to me:

"Above all these stands one great and powerful prince. His name is Kerubiel, a noble and honored leader, full of strength and glory. His power and majesty surpass all others. He is lifted high, a righteous and holy prince, praised in every way.

Thousands of hosts celebrate him, and tens of thousands of armies exalt him. When he is angry, the earth trembles. When he is filled with wrath, the heavens shake. His presence alone causes the foundations of creation to quake, and at his rebuke, even the highest heavens tremble.

His entire body glows with burning coals. His height stretches across the seven heavens, his width spans them completely, and his form is as vast as the entirety of the heavens themselves.

When he opens his mouth, it shines like a fiery lamp, and his tongue blazes like a consuming fire. His eyebrows flash like lightning, his eyes glow with dazzling sparks, and his face burns like a raging fire.

On his head, he wears a crown of holiness, engraved with the sacred Name, from which lightning flashes forth. A divine bow rests between his shoulders. At his waist is a mighty sword, and arrows of blazing fire are strapped to his side. A shield of consuming flames hangs around his neck, surrounded by glowing coals, which encircle him completely.

The brilliance of the Divine Presence shines from his face. Majestic horns rise from his wheels, and a royal diadem rests upon his head.

His entire body is covered in countless eyes, and great wings stretch across his towering form. A burning flame rises on his right, while a fire glows on his left, with coals constantly smoldering. Firebrands erupt from his body, lightning flashes from his face, thunder echoes around him, and earthquakes rumble at his side.

Two powerful princes of the divine chariot remain beside him at all times.

Why is he called Kerubiel? Because he is in charge of the chariot of the Kerubim, the mighty beings under his command. He decorates their crowns and polishes the diadems on their heads.

He enhances their beauty and strengthens their glory. He increases their honor and leads their praise. He magnifies their splendor and refines their radiant majesty. He arranges their songs of worship to prepare a dwelling place for the One who sits upon the Kerubim.

The Kerubim stand beside the Holy Chayyoth, their wings raised high, reaching the tops of their heads. The Divine Presence rests upon them, and the brilliance of Glory shines on their faces. Songs of praise flow from their mouths, their hands are hidden beneath their wings, and their feet are covered as well. Majestic horns rise from their heads, and the light of the Divine Presence radiates from their faces.

Around them are sapphire stones and columns of fire, burning on all four sides. Fiery pillars stand beside them. A sapphire rests on one side and another on the opposite side, with glowing coals beneath them.

In every direction, divine signs stand, while their wings interlock above their heads in a display of majesty. They spread their wings in praise of the One who rides upon the clouds and glorify the awe-inspiring King of Kings.

Kerubiel, the prince who rules over them, arranges them in perfect harmony. He lifts them to new heights of honor and splendor. He strengthens them with power and beauty so they can fulfill the will of their Creator at all times. Above their exalted heads, the glory of the High King, who dwells upon the Kerubim, shines without end."

Chapter XXI (B)

Rabbi Ishmael said: Metatron, the angel, the Prince of the Presence, explained to me:

There is a great court before the Throne of Glory.

How do the angels stand in the heights of heaven? He said: They stand like a vast and endless bridge, stretching as if over a great river. No seraph or angel is assigned to rule over it; all may approach, but the distance to cross it is enormous, measuring 30,000 parasangs. Other bridges, just as massive, extend across countless parasangs, from one end to the other. As it is written in Isaiah 6:2: "And the Seraphim stand above it and proclaim a song before Him."

The last word of this verse has a numerical value of 86, which matches the sacred name YHWH, the God of Israel. Standing before His Throne are powerful and fearsome beings—thousands upon thousands, and ten thousand times ten thousand. They lift their voices in songs of praise and worship before YHWH, the God of Israel.

The sacred text also reveals the number of bridges that exist in the heavens. There are many different kinds: bridges of fire, bridges of hail, and also rivers of hail. There are treasuries of snow and spinning wheels of fire.

There are 24 myriads of these fiery wheels. The ministering angels number 12,000 myriads—6,000 myriads above and 6,000 myriads below. In the same way, there are 12,000 rivers of hail and 12,000 treasuries of snow, equally divided—6,000 above and 6,000 below. The 24 myriads of fiery wheels are also split evenly, 12 above and 12 below. They surround the bridges, the rivers of fire, and the rivers of hail. Many ministering angels create paths through them, guiding all who stand in their midst, aligning their power with the roads of the heavens.

What does YHWH, the God of Israel, the King of Glory, do? The Great and Fearsome One, mighty in strength, hides His face.

In the highest heaven, Araboth, there are 660,000 myriads of glorious angels standing before the Throne of Glory, surrounded by blazing divisions of fire. The King of Glory covers His face, for if He did not, the heavens themselves would be torn apart by the overwhelming brilliance, majesty, beauty, and holiness of the Holy One, blessed be He.

Countless ministering angels carry out His will. There are unnumbered kings and rulers in Araboth, dwelling in His divine presence. These are honored angels among the leaders of the heavens, singing praises and remembering love. They tremble in awe of the splendor of the Divine Presence, their eyes blinded by the shining beauty of their King. Their faces darken, and their strength fades before Him.

From His Throne, rivers of joy pour forth—streams of gladness, rivers of celebration, streams of triumph, rivers of love, and currents of friendship. These waters grow stronger as they flow, surging through the gates of Araboth, carrying a mighty sound. They are accompanied by the voices of the Chayyoth marching and calling out, by the joyful tambourines of the Ophannim, and by the ringing cymbals of the Kerubim.

As these rivers swell, they rise with the song:

"HOLY, HOLY, HOLY IS THE LORD OF HOSTS; THE WHOLE EARTH IS FILLED WITH HIS GLORY."

Chapter XXI (C)

Rabbi Ishmael said: Metatron, the Prince of the Presence, explained to me:

The distance between each bridge is 12 myriads of parasangs. The path leading up spans 12 myriads of parasangs, and the path going down is the same.

The space between the rivers of dread and the rivers of fear is 22 myriads of parasangs. The distance between the rivers of hail and the rivers of darkness is 33 myriads. From the chambers of lightning to the clouds of compassion, it is 42 myriads. The clouds of compassion are 84 myriads away from the divine chariot. From the divine chariot to the Kerubim, the distance is 148 myriads. Between the Kerubim and the Ophannim, there are 24 myriads, and from the Ophannim to the inner chambers, the distance is also 24 myriads. From the inner chambers to the Holy Chayyoth, the span is 100,000 myriads of parasangs.

The space between the wings of the Chayyoth measures 12 myriads, and the width of each wing is the same. The distance between the Holy Chayyoth and the Throne of Glory stretches 130,000 myriads of parasangs.

From the base of the Throne to its seat, there are 40,000 myriads of parasangs. And the name of the One who sits upon it—let His name be made holy!

The arches of the Bow rise high above the heavens, reaching 1,000 thousands and 10,000 times ten thousands of parasangs in height. Their size matches the measure of the Irin and Qaddishin, the Warriors and Holy Ones. As it is written in Genesis 9:13: "My bow I have set in the cloud." It does not say "I will set," but "I have set," meaning it is already placed. These clouds surround the Throne of Glory, and as they pass by, the angels of hail are transformed into burning coals.

The fire of the divine voice descends from the Holy Chayyoth, but because of its power, the Chayyoth run to another place, fearing they might be sent forth. Yet they return quickly, afraid of judgment from the other side. This is why it is said in Ezekiel 1:14, "They run and return."

The arches of the Bow shine more brilliantly than the summer sun at its peak. They glow brighter than blazing fire, and their beauty and radiance have no equal.

Above the arches of the Bow stand the wheels of the Ophannim. Their height measures 1,000 thousands and 10,000 times ten thousands of parasangs, matching the measure of the Seraphim and the Heavenly Troops."

Chapter XXII

The winds blowing under the wings of the Kerubim

Rabbi Ishmael said: Metatron, the angel and Prince of the Presence, explained to me:

"Beneath the wings of the Kerubim, many different winds blow. Among them is the Brooding Wind, as it is written in Genesis 1:2: 'And the wind of God was brooding over the waters.'

There is also the Strong Wind, mentioned in Exodus 14:21: 'And the Lord caused the sea to go back by a strong east wind all that night.'

The East Wind is another, as written in Exodus 10:13: 'The east wind brought the locusts.'

The Wind of Quails is described in Numbers 11:31: 'And there went forth a wind from the Lord and brought quails.'

The Wind of Jealousy is also among them, as mentioned in Numbers 5:14: 'And the wind of jealousy came upon him.'

The Wind of Earthquake appears in 1 Kings 19:11: 'After that came the wind of the earthquake, but the Lord was not in the earthquake.'

The Wind of the Lord is described in Ezekiel 37:1: 'And He carried me out by the wind of the Lord and set me down.'

There is also the Evil Wind, as written in 1 Samuel 16:23: 'And the evil wind departed from him.'

Other winds include the Wind of Wisdom, Wind of Understanding, Wind of Knowledge, and Wind of the Fear of the Lord, as Isaiah 11:2 states: 'And the wind of the Lord shall rest upon him—the wind of wisdom and understanding, the wind of counsel and might, the wind of knowledge and the fear of the Lord.'

The Wind of Rain is found in Proverbs 25:23: 'The north wind brings forth rain.'

The Wind of Lightnings is mentioned in Jeremiah 10:13 and 51:16: 'He makes lightnings for the rain and brings forth the wind out of His treasuries.'

The Wind that Breaks the Rocks is described in 1 Kings 19:11: 'The Lord passed by, and a great and strong wind tore through the mountains and shattered the rocks before the Lord.'

The Wind that Calms the Sea is found in Genesis 8:1: 'And God made a wind pass over the earth, and the waters subsided.'

The Wind of Wrath appears in Job 1:19: 'And behold, there came a great wind from the wilderness, striking the four corners of the house, and it collapsed.'

The Storm-Wind is mentioned in Psalm 148:8: 'Storm-wind, fulfilling His word.'

Satan is also connected to these winds, as Storm-Wind is sometimes linked to him. But all of these winds move only beneath the wings of the Kerubim, as Psalm 18:11 says: 'And He rode upon a cherub and flew; yes, He soared upon the wings of the wind.'

Where do these winds go? Scripture explains that they emerge from beneath the wings of the Kerubim and travel to the globe of the sun, as Ecclesiastes 1:6 states: 'The wind moves toward the south and turns toward the north; it continues its cycle, returning to where it started.'

From the sun, they flow to the rivers and seas, then move across the mountains and hills, as written in Amos 4:13: 'For behold, He who forms the mountains and creates the wind.'

From the mountains and hills, they return to the seas and rivers. From the seas and rivers, they pass over cities and lands. From the cities, they enter the Garden, and from the Garden, they reach Eden, as Genesis 3:8 says: 'Walking in the Garden in the wind of the day.'

Inside the Garden, the winds blend together, moving back and forth. They absorb the fragrance of the spices from every corner of the Garden. Then, they spread out again, carrying this pure scent. This fragrance is brought from the farthest parts of Eden to the righteous, who will one day inherit the Garden of Eden and the Tree of Life, as written in Song of Songs 4:16:

'Awake, O north wind; and come, O south wind! Blow upon my garden, that its spices may flow out. Let my beloved enter his garden and eat its precious fruits.'"

Chapter XXIII

The different chariots of the Holy One, blessed be He

Rabbi Ishmael said: Metatron, the angel and Prince of the Presence, explained to me:

"The Holy One, blessed be He, has many different kinds of chariots.

He has the Chariots of the Kerubim, as written in Psalm 18:11 and 2 Samuel 22:11: 'And He rode upon a cherub and flew.' These chariots are carried by the powerful and glorious Kerubim, who bear the divine presence and swiftly transport Him through the heavens.

He has the Chariots of Wind, as written in Psalm 18:10: 'And He flew swiftly upon the wings of the wind.' These chariots move as fast as the wind, carried by the forces of nature across all creation.

He has the Chariots of the Swift Cloud, as written in Isaiah 19:1: 'Behold, the Lord rides upon a swift cloud.' These chariots travel through the skies on clouds, representing divine majesty and swift judgment.

He has the Chariots of Clouds, as written in Exodus 19:9: 'Lo, I come unto you in a cloud.' Surrounded by clouds of glory, these chariots reveal His presence in mystery and splendor.

He has the Chariots of the Altar, as written in Amos 9:1: 'I saw the Lord standing upon the altar.' These chariots connect heaven and sacred places on earth, where He meets with His people.

He has the Chariots of Ribbotaim, as written in Psalm 68:18: 'The chariots of God are Ribbotaim, thousands upon thousands.' These chariots are surrounded by endless multitudes of angels, showing His unlimited power.

He has the Chariots of the Tent, as written in Deuteronomy 31:1: 'And the Lord appeared in the Tent in a pillar of cloud.' These chariots signify His presence in the Tent of Meeting, where He spoke with His people.

Each of these chariots serves a special purpose, displaying His majesty, strength, and presence as He moves through the heavens and interacts with creation.

He has the Chariots of the Tabernacle, as written in Leviticus: 'And the Lord spoke to him out of the tabernacle.' These chariots reveal His presence within the sacred space of the tabernacle, where He communicates His will.

He has the Chariots of the Mercy Seat, as written in Numbers: 'Then he heard the voice speaking to him from above the mercy seat.' These chariots represent the place where divine mercy and guidance are given.

He has the Chariots of Sapphire Stone, as written in Exodus: 'And under His feet was something like a pavement of sapphire stone.' These chariots shine with the brilliance of sapphire, symbolizing purity and heavenly majesty.

He has the Chariots of Eagles, as written in Exodus: 'I bore you on eagles' wings.' This does not mean actual eagles but refers to the speed and strength of those who carry His presence swiftly and powerfully.

He has the Chariots of Shout, as written in Psalms: 'God has gone up with a shout.' These chariots carry the triumphant and joyful proclamation of His glory through the heavens.

He has the Chariots of Araboth, as written in Psalms: 'Extol Him who rides upon the Araboth.' These chariots exist in the highest heavens, carrying His presence through the exalted realms.

He has the Chariots of Thick Clouds, as written in Psalms: 'He makes the thick clouds His chariot.' These chariots are hidden by clouds, showing the mystery and awe of His presence.

He has the Chariots of the Chayyoth, as written in Ezekiel: 'And the Chayyoth ran and returned.' These chariots, powered by the Holy Chayyoth, only move by divine command, as the Shekinah rests above them.

He has the Chariots of Wheels, as written in Ezekiel: 'And he said: Go in between the whirling wheels.' These chariots, moved by celestial wheels, represent divine power and movement.

He has the Chariots of a Swift Cherub, as written: 'Riding on a swift cherub.' When He rides upon a cherub, He places one foot upon it, and before setting the other foot down, He looks across eighteen thousand worlds. In that single moment, He sees and understands everything within them, as written in Psalms: 'You know my sitting down and my rising up; You understand my thoughts from afar.' Nothing in creation is hidden from Him.

Think of how much He perceives in just that instant, between one step and the next. When He rides upon the cherub and descends, His glory fills all creation. Then He rises again to His place. Everything exists because of His word, as written in Psalms: 'By the word of the Lord, the heavens were made.'

Who can count the number of His chariots? Scripture teaches that all these chariots stand before Him, ready to serve. There are countless myriads upon myriads of them.

The One who rides upon them knows their exact number. He has the power to set His foot upon them, and they bow before Him in complete submission, as written in Psalms: 'If I ascend into heaven, You are there; if I make my bed in the depths, You are there.'

When He rides upon the Kerubim, they carry Him. He moves upon their wings and dwells among them, yet they remain His servants, fulfilling His will.

All these chariots are bound by a divine oath to serve Him. With a single glance, He sees all of creation and rules over it. The chariots move at His command, without hesitation.

When He calls them, they respond instantly. They hear His voice, rush to carry out His will, and glorify the name of the Holy One, blessed be He."

Chapter XXIV

'Ophanniel, the Triune of the 'Ophannim

Rabbi Ishmael said: Metatron, the angel and Prince of the Presence, explained to me:

"Above all these beings, there is a powerful and exalted prince, ancient and mighty. His name is 'Ophanniel.

He has sixteen faces—four on each side—and one hundred wings on each side of his body. His form is covered with 8,466 eyes, matching the number of days in the year.

Each of his two front-facing eyes flashes with lightning, and from them, flames erupt. No creature can look directly at his eyes, because anyone who tries is instantly consumed by their intense fire.

His height is so vast that it would take 2,500 years to travel its full distance. No one can fully comprehend his size, and no words can describe his great strength—only the King of kings, the Holy One, blessed be He, knows the full extent of his power.

Why is he called 'Ophanniel? Because he is in charge of the 'Ophannim, and they have been placed under his care. Every day, he stands to serve them. He enhances their beauty, organizes their chambers, polishes their foundations, refines their dwellings, smooths their edges, and cleanses their seats. He tends to them day and night, making sure they shine with splendor, stand with dignity, and are always prepared to offer praise to their Creator.

The 'Ophannim are covered in countless eyes, and their radiance shines in every direction. On the right side of their garments, seventy-two sapphire stones are placed, and another seventy-two sapphire stones decorate the left side.

Each 'Ophan wears a crown set with four glowing carbuncle stones. These stones shine in all four directions of the highest heaven, just as the light of the sun spreads across the entire universe. Why are they called carbuncle stones? Because their brilliance resembles flashing lightning.

The 'Ophannim are surrounded by magnificent tents made of sapphire and carbuncle, glowing with splendor and brilliance. These tents shield them and intensify the dazzling beauty of their shining eyes, filling the space around them with an unmatched, radiant glow."

Chapter XXV

Seraphiel, the Prince of the Seraphim

Rabbi Ishmael said: Metatron, the angel and Prince of the Presence, explained to me:

"Above all these beings stands a powerful and magnificent prince. He is extraordinary in every way—great, noble, honored, mighty, and awe-inspiring. He leads the heavenly hosts, moves with incredible speed, and is a scribe of unmatched skill. He is glorified, deeply respected, and loved by all.

His entire being radiates with splendor, shining with light and brilliance. Every part of him reflects beauty and greatness.

His face glows like that of angels, but his body is shaped like a mighty eagle.

His radiance flashes like lightning, his appearance burns like fire, and his beauty shines like the brightest stars. His glory glows like burning coals, his majesty sparkles like polished metal, and his brilliance resembles the glow of the planet Venus. His form reflects the light of the sun, and his height reaches the full span of the seven heavens. The light from his eyebrows is seven times brighter than normal light.

A massive sapphire stone rests on his head, as large as the entire universe, shining as brilliantly as the heavens themselves.

His entire body is covered with countless eyes, as numerous as the stars in the sky. Each eye shines like Venus, though some glow like the moon and others like the sun. Different parts of his body radiate different types of light:

- From his ankles to his knees, his glow is like flashing stars.
- From his knees to his thighs, it shines like Venus.
- From his thighs to his waist, it mirrors the brightness of the moon.
- From his waist to his neck, it radiates like the sun.
- From his neck to his head, it shines with a light that never fades.

The crown on his head is as brilliant as the Throne of Glory itself. Its size covers a distance that would take 200 years to travel. Upon this crown rests every kind of radiance, glow, and brilliance found in the universe.

This prince's name is Seraphiel, and the crown he wears is called the Prince of Peace. He is named Seraphiel because he is in charge of the Seraphim, the fiery beings under his care. Day and night, he watches over them, teaches them songs of praise, and guides them in exalting the beauty, power, and majesty of the King. He helps them sanctify His name with the greatest reverence.

The Seraphim are four in number, representing the four winds of the world. Each one has six wings, symbolizing the six days of Creation. They each have four faces.

Their size is beyond imagination—each Seraph is as tall as the seven heavens combined. Each wing is as wide as the entire sky, and each face is as vast as the whole eastern horizon.

The Seraphim shine with a light so intense that it rivals the brightness of the Throne of Glory. Their glow is so overwhelming that even the Holy Chayyoth, the mighty Ophannim, and the majestic Kerubim cannot look at them. Anyone who dares to gaze at them is instantly blinded by their incredible brilliance.

They are called Seraphim because they burn (saraph) the writing tables of Satan. Each day, Satan, along with Sammael, the Prince of Rome, and Dubbiel, the Prince of Persia, writes down the sins of Israel on tablets. These records are handed over to the Seraphim to present before the Holy One, blessed be He, in an attempt to accuse Israel.

But the Seraphim, knowing the hidden will of the Holy One, blessed be He, understand that He does not desire Israel's destruction. So what do they do? Every day, they take Satan's records and burn them in the flames that blaze before the Throne of Glory. By doing this, they ensure that these accusations never reach the Holy One, especially when He sits upon the Throne of Judgment to judge the world in truth."

Chapter XXVI

Radweriel, the Keeper of the Book of Records

Rabbi Ishmael said: Metatron, the Angel of the Lord and Prince of the Presence, explained to me:

"Above the Seraphim stands a prince of incredible greatness, higher than all other princes and more wondrous than any other heavenly being. His name is Radweriel, and he is responsible for guarding the treasuries of the sacred books.

Radweriel's main duty is to bring forth the Case of Writings, which holds the Book of Records. He retrieves this case and presents it before the Holy One, blessed be He. Once there, he breaks its seals, carefully opens it, and takes out the books inside.

These sacred writings are then placed before the Holy One, blessed be He.

The Holy One, blessed be He, receives the books from Radweriel's hands and gives them to the heavenly scribes, whose job is to read them. This takes place in the Great Beth Din, the divine court in the highest heaven, in front of the entire heavenly assembly.

Why is he called Radweriel? His name reflects a unique and amazing ability—every word that comes from his mouth creates an angel. These angels are formed by the power of his voice and immediately join the ranks of the ministering angels, becoming part of the heavenly choirs.

When the time comes for the Thrice Holy song to be sung, Radweriel takes his place among the singing angels. He lifts his voice in praise, joining the celestial hosts as they glorify their Creator together."

Chapter XXVII

Description of a class of angels

Rabbi Ishmael said: Metatron, the Angel, the Prince of the Presence, explained to me:

Each angel is given seventy names, matching the seventy languages spoken throughout the world. All of these names come from the holy and exalted name of the Holy One, blessed be He. Every name is engraved in fire on the Fearful Crown, which rests upon the head of the high and glorious King.

From each name inscribed on this crown, sparks and flashes of lightning burst forth, filling the heavens with brilliant light. Surrounding each angel are majestic horns of splendor, forming a magnificent display around them. From these horns, streams of light shine outward, creating an endless glow.

Each angel is wrapped in tents of shimmering brightness, their light so intense and overwhelming that even the powerful Seraphim and mighty Chayyoth—greater than all other heavenly beings—cannot look at them. The radiance surrounding these angels is beyond imagination, a reflection of the infinite majesty of the Holy One, blessed be He, from whom their light and strength flow.

Chapter XXVIII

The 'Irin and Qaddishin

Rabbi Ishmael said: Metatron, the Angel, the Prince of the Presence, explained to me:

Above all the heavenly beings stand four great princes, known as the 'Irin and Qaddishin. These princes are highly honored, deeply respected, beloved, and full of glory. They are greater than all other heavenly beings, and no other celestial rulers or servants can compare to them. Each of these four princes is as powerful as all the others combined.

Their dwelling place is directly across from the Throne of Glory, and they stand before the Holy One, blessed be He. The brilliance of their presence reflects the light of the Throne of Glory, and their splendor mirrors the radiance of the Divine Presence.

They are glorified by the majesty of the Divine and praised in the light of the Shekina.

Not only are they deeply revered, but the Holy One, blessed be He, does nothing in the world without first consulting them. Only after seeking their guidance does He act, as it is written in Daniel 4:7: "The sentence is by the decree of the 'Irin and the demand by the word of the Qaddishin."

There are two 'Irin and two Qaddishin. How do they stand before the Holy One, blessed be He? One 'Ir stands on one side, and the other on the opposite side. Likewise, one Qaddish stands on one side, and the other on the opposite side.

These powerful princes lift up the humble and bring down the proud. They raise those who are lowly to great heights and humble the arrogant, lowering them to the dust.

Each day, when the Holy One, blessed be He, sits on the Throne of Judgment to judge the entire world, the Books of the Living and the Books of the Dead are opened before Him. All the heavenly beings stand in fear, awe, and trembling. As He sits upon the Throne of Judgment, His garments shine as white as snow, the hair on His head is as pure as wool, and His entire cloak glows with radiant light. His righteousness covers Him like armor.

The 'Irin and Qaddishin stand before Him like court officers before a judge. They bring cases forward, debate the issues, and bring each matter to a close before the Holy One, blessed be He, as it is written in Daniel 4:17: "The sentence is by the decree of the 'Irin and the demand by the word of the Qaddishin."

Some of them present arguments, while others issue rulings in the Great Beth Din in the highest heaven. Some request decisions from the Divine Majesty, while others finalize the cases presented before the Most High. Others descend to earth to carry out the judgments that have been declared, as it is written in Daniel 4:13-14:

"Behold, an 'Ir and a Qaddish came down from heaven and cried aloud, saying: Cut down the tree and remove its branches, shake off its leaves, and scatter its fruit. Let the animals flee from beneath it, and the birds from its branches."

Why are they called 'Irin and Qaddishin? Because they purify both body and spirit with fiery discipline on the third day of judgment, as it is written in Hosea 6:2:

"After two days, He will revive us. On the third day, He will raise us up, and we shall live before Him."

Chapter XXIX

The 72 Princes of Kingdoms and the Prince of the World officiating at the Great Sanhedrin in heaven

Rabbi Ishmael said: Metatron, the angel and Prince of the Presence, explained to me:

Whenever the Great Court gathers in the highest heavens, no one in the world is allowed to speak—except for a select group of extraordinary princes who have the honor of carrying the name of the Holy One, blessed be He.

How many of these princes are there? There are seventy-two, each one representing a different kingdom on earth. Above them all stands the Prince of the World, who speaks on behalf of all creation. Every day, this great Prince pleads for the world before the Holy One, blessed be He.

This takes place at the sacred moment when the Book of Records is opened. In this book, every action in the world is written down, ready for judgment. As it is written in Daniel 7:10: "The judgment was set, and the books were opened."

At this solemn time, the seventy-two princes and the Prince of the World stand before the Holy One, offering their petitions and arguments. Their purpose is to seek balance and mercy, ensuring that divine justice is carried out with compassion in the highest court of heaven.

Chapter XXX

The attributes of Justice, Mercy, and Truth by the throne of judgment

Rabbi Ishmael said: Metatron, the angel and Prince of the Presence, explained to me:

When the Holy One, blessed be He, sits on the Throne of Judgment to make decisions, three powerful forces stand around Him. Justice is on His right, representing fairness and doing what is right. Mercy is on His left, shining with kindness and compassion. Truth stands directly in front of Him, glowing with honesty and purity.

When a person comes before Him for judgment, something remarkable happens. A staff of light emerges from the glow of Mercy and moves in front of the person. This staff is a sign that compassion is present, even in the face of judgment.

At that moment, the person falls to the ground in humility and awe. The angels of destruction, who are there to carry out punishments, tremble with fear and cannot approach because the power of Mercy is too strong.

As it is written in Isaiah 16:5: "With mercy, the throne will be established, and He will sit upon it in truth." This verse shows how justice and compassion work together on the Throne of the Holy One, blessed be He. Mercy softens judgment, ensuring that decisions are fair and true while also offering hope and redemption to those who come before Him.

Chapter XXXI

The execution of judgement on the wicked. God's sword

Rabbi Ishmael said: Metatron, the angel and Prince of the Presence, told me:

When the Holy One, blessed be He, opens the Book of Records—a divine book made of fire and flame—His judgment begins. From His presence, commands are constantly sent out, ensuring that justice is carried out against the wicked. This is done through His sword, which is drawn from its sheath.

The sword shines as brightly as lightning, and its brilliance spreads across the entire world, lighting up everything from one end of the earth to the other. As it is written in Isaiah: "For by fire, the Lord will judge, and by His sword, all flesh."

The sight of this sword fills everyone on earth with fear and trembling. Its sharp blade flashes like lightning, stretching across the horizon. Sparks and bursts of light, as bright as the stars, shoot from the sword, adding to the overwhelming power it displays. As it is written in Deuteronomy: "If I sharpen the lightning of My sword."

Chapter XXXII

When the Holy One, blessed be He, sits on the Throne of Judgment, different groups of angels take their places around Him. The angels of Mercy stand on His right, showing compassion and speaking on behalf of those being judged. On His left are the angels of Peace, radiating calm and tranquility. Directly in front of Him are the angels of Destruction, ready to carry out His commands as He sees fit.

Beneath the Throne of Glory, a scribe records everything happening in the heavenly court. Another scribe stands above the

Throne, writing down the divine decrees spoken by the Holy One, blessed be He.

Surrounding the Throne on all four sides are the Seraphim, powerful beings made of fire. Their presence forms walls of light and flames that enclose the divine seat. The Ophannim also encircle the Throne, their fiery bodies covered in flames that shine in all directions. To the right and left of the Throne, there are clouds of fire, adding to the incredible majesty of the scene.

Beneath the Throne, the Holy Chayyoth carry it, each with three enormous fingers. The size of each finger is immense, measuring 800,000 and 70 times 100, plus 66,000 parasangs. These mighty beings stand in a breathtaking display of divine power, their strength holding up the Throne of Glory.

Under the feet of the Chayyoth, seven fiery rivers flow endlessly. Each river stretches 3,500 thousand parasangs wide and plunges 248 thousand myriads of parasangs deep. Their length is beyond comprehension, impossible to measure. These rivers curve and flow in all four directions of Araboth, their power spreading across the heavens.

From Araboth, the rivers descend to Mâ'ân, where they pause before moving on to Zebul, then to Shechagim, then to Raqia', and finally to Shamayim. From there, the rivers pour down upon the heads of the wicked in Gehenna, delivering divine judgment. As it is written in Jeremiah 33:19:

"Behold, a whirlwind of the Lord, even His fury, has gone forth, a whirling tempest; it shall burst upon the head of the wicked."

Chapter XXXIII

Rabbi Ishmael said: Metatron, the angel and Prince of the Presence, explained to me:

The feet of the Chayyoth are surrounded by seven layers of burning coals, each glowing with intense heat. Beyond these coals are seven walls of fire, their flames flickering and lighting up everything around them.

Outside these fiery walls are seven layers of hailstones, known as the stones of 'Elgabish, as described in Ezekiel. These hailstones shine with an icy glow, creating a sharp contrast to the fire within. Surrounding them is another layer of hailstones, called the stones of Bârâd, adding yet another powerful barrier.

Beyond these stones are layers of stormy winds, known as the wings of the tempest, swirling with uncontrollable energy. Further out, layers of flames roar fiercely, consuming everything in their path.

These flames are surrounded by the chambers of the whirlwind, constantly spinning and churning. Beyond these chambers are the realms of fire and water, two opposing elements that exist together in perfect balance, sustained by divine power.

Encircling the realms of fire and water are angels who never stop proclaiming "Holy!" as they lift their voices in praise. Beyond them are those who chant "Blessed!" in perfect harmony, their voices echoing throughout the heavens.

Surrounding the singers of "Blessed!" are glowing clouds, radiant with divine light. These clouds are enclosed by burning juniper coals, their heat intense and unrelenting. Around the juniper coals are a thousand camps of fire and ten thousand hosts of flames, each burning with incredible brightness.

Between each camp and host lies a protective cloud, shielding the heavenly beings from the overwhelming fire. These clouds act as a divine barrier, allowing the angels to fulfill their sacred duties and continue their endless worship of the Holy One, blessed be He.

Chapter XXXIV

Rabbi Ishmael said: The angel Metatron, the Prince of the Presence, explained to me:

In the highest heaven, called Araboth Raqia', God created an enormous number of angels—506,000 groups in total. Each group has 49,000 angels, and they are incredibly powerful and awe-inspiring.

Each angel is as vast as the ocean. Their faces shine as bright as lightning, their eyes glow like fire, and their arms and legs gleam like polished metal. When they speak, their voices boom like a mighty roar, full of strength and majesty.

All of these angels stand before God's Throne of Glory in four enormous rows. Each row is led by powerful angelic commanders who guide them with authority and dedication.

Some angels spend their time calling out "Holy!" while others say "Blessed!" Some act as swift messengers, rushing to carry out God's commands, while others remain still, standing in deep respect before Him. As it says in the Book of Daniel:

"Thousands upon thousands served Him, and ten thousand times ten thousand stood before Him. The court was seated, and the books were opened."

When it is time to declare the Kedushsha—the sacred praise of God—a great whirlwind suddenly bursts forth from before Him. This storm moves through the Camp of Shekhinah, shaking the heavens, just as it is written in Jeremiah:

"Look! The whirlwind of the Lord goes out in fury, a raging storm."

In that moment, thousands of angels transform into flashes of fire, streaks of lightning, and bursts of energy. Some turn into flames, rushing winds, or blazing fires. Others take the shape of glowing figures, shining like living sparks of light.

These changes happen because they fully submit to God's power. They tremble with awe and fear, overwhelmed by His presence.

They stay in this state of intense motion and energy until they completely embrace their purpose—to praise the glorious King. Once they do, they return to their original forms, standing strong and devoted. Their focus never shifts from singing praises to God, just as it says in Isaiah:

"And one called to another and said: Holy, Holy, Holy is the Lord of Hosts; the whole earth is filled with His glory."

Chapter XXXV

The angels bathe in the fiery river before reciting the Song

Rabbi Ishmael said: Metatron, the Angel, the Prince of the Presence, explained to me:

When the angels get ready to sing their Song of Praise, a powerful river of fire, called Nehar diNur, rises up, glowing with intense energy. This blazing river is filled with countless angels, each radiating strength and divine fire. It flows beneath God's Throne of Glory, passing between the angels' camps and the vast ranks of 'Araboth.

Before they can begin their song, the angels must first enter this fiery river. Each one fully immerses themselves in the flames, cleansing their spirit and preparing for the sacred task ahead. They dip their entire bodies into the fire, then carefully purify their tongues and mouths seven times, making sure their words are worthy of being offered to God.

Once purified, they emerge from the river and dress in shining robes of Machage Samal, glowing with purity and beauty. Over these, they wrap themselves in shimmering cloaks of chashmal, radiating divine light. Clothed in this sacred attire, they take their places in four perfect rows before the Throne of Glory.

This holy gathering stretches across all the heavens, with every angel standing ready to sing. In their purified state, they reflect the greatness and holiness of their Creator, prepared to lift their voices in perfect harmony to praise Him.

Chapter XXXVI

The four camps of Shekina and their surroundings

Rabbi Ishmael said: The angel Metatron, the Prince of the Presence, explained to me:

Inside the seven heavenly halls, there are four magnificent chariots of Shekina, each shining with divine glory. In front of every chariot stand four great groups of Shekina's celestial army, filled with unmatched beauty and holiness. Flowing between these groups is a mighty river of fire, burning endlessly, symbolizing the eternal power of God's presence.

Surrounding the fiery rivers are glowing clouds, casting a soft, sacred light across the heavens. Between these clouds rise towering pillars of brimstone, standing strong as symbols of divine power and purity. Around each pillar, flaming wheels spin in endless motion, forming brilliant circles of fire.

Between these fiery wheels, flames blaze continuously, never fading. Within these flames are great treasuries of lightning, bursting with dazzling flashes that light up the heavens with awe. Beyond the lightning are the mighty wings of the storm wind, always moving, carrying out God's will across the universe.

Behind these powerful winds are the chambers of the storm, where the wild forces of nature gather and are held in place. Beyond these chambers lie vast realms filled with roaring winds, echoing voices, rolling thunder, and endless bursts of sparks. Layer upon layer, earthquakes rumble behind them, shaking one after another, their force revealing the unshakable power of the Holy One.

This breathtaking and intricate arrangement reflects divine order, with each element playing its role in upholding the chariots and the heavenly hosts of Shekina—eternal signs of God's infinite glory and rule.

Chapter XXXVII

The fear that befalls all the heavens at the sound of the Holy, especially the heavenly bodies, and their appeasement by the Prince of the World

Rabbi Ishmael said: The angel Metatron, the Prince of the Presence, explained to me:

Within the seven heavenly halls, there are four majestic chariots of Shekina, each glowing with divine light. In front of these chariots stand four great groups of Shekina's celestial army, filled with beauty and holiness beyond imagination. Flowing between these groups is a powerful river of fire, burning without end, representing the everlasting presence of God.

Surrounding this fiery river are bright, glowing clouds that spread a soft, sacred light. Between them rise towering pillars of brimstone, standing firm as symbols of divine strength and purity. Around each pillar, spinning wheels of fire create endless, dazzling circles of light.

Between these fiery wheels, flames burn without stopping. Inside these flames are great stores of lightning, sending out brilliant flashes that fill the heavens with awe. Beyond the lightning, the mighty wings of the storm winds move without rest, carrying out God's will across creation.

Behind these powerful winds are the chambers of the storm, where the forces of nature are gathered and held. Beyond them stretch vast realms filled with rushing winds, echoing voices, rolling thunder, and endless bursts of sparks. Layer after layer, earthquakes shake the space behind them, one trembling after another, revealing the unstoppable power of the Holy One.

This incredible and intricate structure reflects the divine order, with each part playing its role in upholding the chariots and the heavenly hosts of Shekina—eternal symbols of God's endless glory and rule.

Chapter XXXVIII

The explicit names fly off from the Throne, and all the various angelic hosts prostrate themselves before it during the Qedushsha

Rabbi Ishmael said: The angel Metatron, the Prince of the Presence, explained to me:

When the angels begin to chant "Holy," something incredible happens. The sacred names of God, written in fiery letters on the Throne of Glory, suddenly take flight. These powerful names rise into the sky like mighty eagles, each one shining with divine energy. They are carried by sixteen wings and soar together, circling around the Holy One on all sides of His divine presence.

As this sacred moment unfolds, all the angels and heavenly beings watch in awe. The radiant angels join with the fiery Servants, the powerful Ophannim, and the Kerubim of Shekina. The shining Chayyoth stand alongside the Seraphim, the 'Er'ellim, and the

Mephsarim. Armies of fire, blazing with intense flames, gather in deep worship.

The holy princes, wearing crowns of glory, stand in robes that shine like royal garments. Their very beings radiate strength and splendor. In complete humility, they bow before God, lowering themselves three times in perfect harmony.

Their voices rise together, filling the heavens with a powerful declaration: "Blessed be the name of His glorious kingdom forever and ever." Their worship reflects the unity of creation, the purpose of their existence, and their deep reverence for the One who rules over all.

Chapter XXXIX

The ministering angels rewarded with crowns for properly uttering the "Holy," and consumed by fire for failing, with new ones created to take their place

Rabbi Ishmael said: The angel Metatron, the Prince of the Presence, explained to me:

When the angels chant "Holy" before God with the right order and deep respect, a moment of divine joy fills the heavens. The attendants of His Throne of Glory step forward, emerging with great happiness. Each of them carries countless crowns—thousands upon thousands, shining brightly like the planet Venus.

These crowns are given to the angels and the great heavenly princes who proclaim "Holy." Each one receives three crowns: the first for saying "Holy," the second for saying "Holy, Holy," and the third for completing the chant with "Holy, Holy, Holy is the Lord of Hosts." This act shows God's approval and pleasure, recognizing their devotion and place in the heavenly order.

However, if the angels fail to say "Holy" in the correct way or without proper focus, a blazing fire bursts from the little finger of

God. This fire rushes into their ranks, splitting into 496,000 flames, each one directed at the four great camps of the angels. In a single moment, those who made mistakes are consumed by the flames, as it is written: "A fire goes before Him and burns up His enemies all around."

But immediately after, God speaks a single word, and from that word, new angels are created to take the place of those who were lost. These newly formed angels stand before the Throne of Glory and join in the never-ending song of praise, declaring "Holy" without hesitation. As it is written: "They are new every morning; great is Your faithfulness." Each day, fresh and renewed angels rise to continue the eternal worship of God.

Chapter XL

Metatron shows R. Ishmael the letters engraved on the Throne of Glory, by which all of creation was made

R. Ishmael said: Metatron, the Angel, the Prince of the Presence, spoke to me and said:

Come and see the letters that shaped the heavens and the earth—the same letters that formed the mountains and hills. These are the letters that created the seas and rivers, the trees, and every plant that grows on the land. They are the letters that brought the planets and stars into existence, setting the sun, moon, and great constellations like Orion and the Pleiades into their places, filling the sky with light.

These same letters were used to create the Throne of Glory, the spinning Wheels of the Merkaba, and everything needed to sustain the universe. Through them, wisdom, understanding, and knowledge came to be. They also formed virtues like patience, humility, and righteousness, which keep the world in balance.

As I walked beside him, he held my hand and lifted me onto his wings. He showed me these sacred letters, each one carved in flames upon the Throne of Glory. Sparks flew from them, their light spreading out and filling all the chambers of 'Araboth, shining across the highest heavens with their brilliance.

Chapter XLI

R. Ishmael said: Metatron, the Angel, the Prince of the Presence, said to me:

Come, and I will show you where amazing things happen. I will take you to the place where water is suspended high above, where fire burns inside hail but is never put out, where lightning flashes from snowy mountains, where thunder echoes in the highest heavens, where flames burn inside other flames, and where powerful voices sound through thunder and earthquakes.

As we walked, he took my hand and lifted me onto his wings, showing me all these wonders. I saw the waters held high in 'Araboth Raqia', kept in place by the power of the name YAH 'EHYEH ASHER 'EHYEH (I Am That I Am). From these waters, streams flowed down to the earth, nourishing it, just as it is written: "He waters the mountains from His chambers; the earth is satisfied with the fruit of His works."

I also saw fire and snow side by side, neither harming the other, kept in perfect balance by the power of the name 'ESHK 'OKLA (Consuming Fire), as it is written: "For the Lord your God is a consuming fire."

I watched as flashes of lightning shot out from snowy mountains, yet they did not fade, sustained by the power of the name YAH TSUR OLAMIM (The Everlasting Rock), as it is written: "For in Jah, the Lord, is an everlasting rock."

I heard roaring thunder and mighty voices rising from fiery flames, their sound never fading, held strong by the power of the name 'EL SHADDAI RABBA (The Great God Almighty), as it is written: "I am God Almighty."

I saw flames glowing brightly inside other flames, burning without being consumed, upheld by the power of the name CAD AL KES YAH (The Hand Upon the Throne of the Lord), as it is written: "For the hand is upon the Throne of the Lord."

I witnessed rivers of fire flowing alongside rivers of water, yet neither one destroyed the other. They remained in harmony through the power of the name OSEH SHALOM (Maker of Peace), as it is written: "He makes peace in His high places." For it is He who creates peace between fire and water, hail and flame, wind and cloud, earthquake and sparks.

Chapter XLII

Metatron shows R. Ishmael the abode of the unborn spirits and of the spirits of the righteous dead

R. Ishmael said: Metatron said to me:

"Come, and I will show you where the spirits of the righteous are—those who have already lived and returned, as well as those who have not yet been born."

He brought me close, took my hand, and lifted me up near the Throne of Glory, the place where the Shekina dwells. There, he revealed the Throne of Glory to me, and I saw the spirits that had lived and returned. They were soaring above the throne, in the presence of the Holy One.

Then, I reflected on a verse from Scripture and found its meaning in what is written: "For the spirit clothed itself before me, and the souls I have made" (Isaiah 57:16). The words "for the spirit clothed itself before me" refer to the spirits that were created in the chamber of creation for the righteous and have returned to God. The phrase "the souls I have made" refers to the spirits of the righteous who have not yet been born and remain in a chamber known as GUPH.

Chapter XLIII

Metatron shows R. Ishmael the abode of the wicked and the intermediate in Sheol. (vss. 1–6)

The Patriarchs pray for the deliverance of Israel (vss. 7–10)

R. Ishmael said: Metatron, the Angel, the Prince of the Presence, said to me:

"Come, and I will show you where the spirits of the wicked and those in between dwell, where they stand, and where they are taken. I will show you where the in-between spirits descend and where the wicked are cast down."

He said to me, "Two angels of destruction, Za'aphiel and Simkiel, send the spirits of the wicked to Sheol."

Simkiel is responsible for the in-between spirits, guiding and purifying them because of the great mercy of Adonai, the Prince of the Place. Za'aphiel is in charge of the wicked, driving them away from God's presence and the splendor of the Shekina. They are sent to Sheol to be punished in the fire of Gehenna, beaten with rods of burning coal.

As we walked, he took my hand and pointed out everything with his fingers.

I saw their faces—they looked human, but their bodies were like eagles. The spirits of those in between had a pale grey appearance because of their actions. Their sins left marks on them until they were cleansed by fire.

The faces of the wicked, however, were as black as the bottom of a pot, showing the depth of their evil and the wrongs they had done.

Then I saw the spirits of the Patriarchs—Abraham, Isaac, and Jacob—along with the spirits of the righteous. They had risen from their graves and ascended to the Heaven of Raqia'. Standing before God, they prayed with sorrow in their voices:

"Lord of the Universe, how much longer will You remain on Your Throne in mourning, with Your right hand held back? When will You rescue Your children and reveal Your Kingdom to the world? How much longer will You leave Your people as slaves among the nations? When will You show mercy once more? The hand with which You stretched out the heavens and the earth—when will You raise it again in compassion?"

God answered them, saying, "How can I act while the wicked continue to sin so terribly? How can I lift My mighty right hand when their wrongdoing has caused such destruction?"

At that moment, Metatron turned to me and said, "My servant, take the books and read their deeds!" I took the books and read the records of their actions. Every wicked soul had broken the Torah in every possible way, disobeying every law and commandment. As it is written, "Yes, all Israel has transgressed Your Law" (Daniel 9:11). The word was not written as toratecha but torateka, meaning they had violated every letter of the Torah, from the first (Aleph) to the last (Tav). Each letter of the Torah stood as a witness against them.

Upon hearing this, Abraham, Isaac, and Jacob wept bitterly. Then God said to them, "Abraham, My beloved; Isaac, My chosen one; Jacob, My firstborn—how can I now rescue these people from the hands of the nations?"

At that moment, Mihmael, the Prince of Israel, cried out in grief, weeping loudly, and said, "Why do You stand far off, O Lord?" (Psalm 10:1).

Chapter XLIV

Metatron shows R. Ishmael last and future events recorded on the Curtain of the Throne

R. Ishmael said: Metatron said to me:

"Come, and I will show you the Curtain of MAQOM, where the Divine Majesty is displayed. On it, every generation of the world is recorded—all their actions, past and future, until the end of time."

He took me with him, pointing things out with his fingers, like a father teaching his child to read the Torah. I saw every generation and its leaders:

- The rulers and heads of each generation
- The guides and shepherds
- The oppressors and those in power
- The protectors and guardians
- The judges and court officials
- The teachers and supporters
- The noblemen and warriors
- The elders and counselors

I saw Adam and his generation, their deeds and thoughts.

I saw Noah and his generation, their choices and actions.

I saw those who lived before the flood, their behavior and their fate.

I saw Shem and Nimrod, and the generation of the Tower of Babel, their struggles and their beliefs.

I saw Abraham, Isaac, and Ishmael—each with their own generation and their deeds.

I saw Jacob, Joseph, and the twelve tribes, their lives and their journeys.

I saw Moses and his people, Aaron, Miriam, the elders, and the leaders of Israel.

Then Metatron spoke:

"I saw Joshua and his generation, their victories and failures.

I saw the judges of Israel, their wisdom and struggles.

I saw Eli, Phinehas, and Samuel, and how they led their people.

I saw the kings of Judah and Israel, the choices they made, and their impact on history.

I saw the princes of Israel and the rulers of other nations, their ambitions and their deeds.

I saw the heads of councils in Israel and the nations, their leadership and decisions.

I saw the nobles, the judges, and the wise men—both of Israel and the other nations.

I saw the teachers of children in Israel and across the world, shaping the next generations.

I saw the prophets of Israel and the prophets of the nations, their messages and warnings.

I witnessed every war and battle that the nations fought against Israel during its time as a kingdom.

I saw the Messiah, the son of Joseph, and his generation, their actions, and their struggles against the nations.

I saw the Messiah, the son of David, and his time—his battles, his triumphs, and his hardships alongside Israel.

I saw the great wars of Gog and Magog in the days of the Messiah, and everything that God will do in those times.

I saw every leader, every generation, and every event—both in Israel and among the nations. Everything that has happened and everything that will take place until the end of time was written on the Curtain of MAQOM.

I saw it all with my own eyes. After witnessing these things, I opened my mouth to praise MAQOM, saying:

"For the King's word has power, and who may say to Him, 'What are You doing?'" (Ecclesiastes 8:4).

"O Lord, how great are Your works!" (Psalm 104:24).

Chapter XLV

The place of the stars shown to R. Ishmael

R. Ishmael said: Metatron said to me:

"Come, and I will show you where the stars rest, where they stand each night in the sky, filled with awe for MAQOM, and where they move from their places of rest."

I walked beside him as he took my hand, pointing out everything with his fingers. I saw the stars standing on sparks of blazing fire, surrounding the Chariot of the Almighty. Then Metatron clapped his hands, and the stars were set into motion. Instantly, they shot into the sky on fiery wings, scattering in all directions from the Throne of the Merkaba. As they soared, Metatron spoke the name of each one to me, fulfilling what is written: "He counts the number of the stars; He gives each one its name" (Psalm 147:4). This shows that the Holy One has given every star a unique name.

With perfect order, each star follows Haniel into the heavens, Raqia' hashamayim, to serve the world. When their task is done, they return in the same way to sing praises to the Holy One through songs and hymns, as it is written: "The heavens declare the glory of God" (Psalm 19:1).

In the future, the Holy One will make them new again, as it is written: "They are new every morning" (Lamentations 3:23). Then, they will open their mouths to sing a song of praise. What will they sing? It is written: "When I consider Your heavens..." (Psalm 8:3).

Chapter XLVI

Metatron shows R. Ishmael the spirits of the punished angels

R. Ishmael said: Metatron said to me:

"Come, and I will show you the souls of the angels and the spirits of the heavenly servants whose bodies have been burned by the fire of MAQOM (the Almighty). This fire comes from His little finger. These angels have been turned into fiery coals within the River of Fire (Nehar diNur), but their spirits and souls remain behind the Shekina, standing in eternal reverence.

Whenever the heavenly servants sing at the wrong time or in a way that was not commanded, they are consumed by the fire of their Creator. A flame sent by God burns them up within the chambers of the whirlwind. This mighty wind sweeps them away, casting them into the River of Fire, where they are transformed into great mountains of burning coal. However, their spirits and souls always return to their Creator, continuing to stand behind Him in devotion.

I walked beside Metatron as he took my hand and led me to see these spirits and souls. He showed me where they stood behind the Shekina, resting on the wings of the whirlwind and surrounded by walls of fire.

Then Metatron opened the gates of the fiery walls where these spirits remained behind the Shekina. I looked up and saw them. They had the forms of angels, and their wings were like those of birds, but made entirely of flames, created from burning fire.

In that moment, I opened my mouth and praised MAQOM, saying: 'How great are Your works, O Lord!' (Psalm 92:3)."

Chapter XLVII (A)

Metatron shows R. Ishmael the Right Hand of the Most High, now inactive behind Him, but in the future destined to work the deliverance of Israel

R. Ishmael said: Metatron said to me:

"Come, and I will show you the Right Hand of MAQOM, which has been placed behind Him since the destruction of the Holy Temple. From it shines every kind of light and splendor, and through it, the 955 heavens were created. Even the seraphim and Ophannim are not allowed to look at it until the day of salvation arrives.

I walked beside him, and he took my hand. With joy, songs, and praise, he showed me the Right Hand of MAQOM. No words can fully describe its beauty, and no eyes can withstand its greatness, majesty, and glory.

By its side stand the souls of the righteous, those found worthy to witness the joy of Jerusalem. They praise and pray before it three times a day, saying, "Awake, awake, put on strength, O arm of the Lord." As it is written: "He caused His glorious arm to go at the right hand of Moses."

At that moment, the Right Hand of MAQOM was weeping. From its five fingers, five rivers of tears flowed down into the great sea, shaking the entire world. This is as written in Scripture: "The earth is utterly broken, the earth is torn apart, the earth shakes violently. The earth will stagger like a drunken man and sway like a hut." These five events are connected to the five fingers of His mighty hand.

When the Holy One sees that there is no righteous person left in the generation, no one devoted to goodness, and no justice among people—when there is no one like Moses or Samuel to stand before Him and pray for salvation and deliverance—when no one calls upon His Right Hand to act on behalf of Israel, then He remembers His own justice, mercy, and grace. By His own power, He will bring salvation. As it is written:

"He saw that there was no one, and He was amazed that there was no one to intercede; so His own arm brought salvation, and His righteousness upheld Him."

Scripture reminds us how Moses constantly prayed for Israel in the wilderness, preventing divine judgment, and how Samuel called upon God, who answered his prayers, even when they were not part of the divine plan. As it is written: "Moses and Aaron were among His priests" and "Even if Moses and Samuel stood before Me."

At that time, the Holy One will say: "How long shall I wait for humanity to bring salvation through their righteousness? For My own sake, for My merit and justice, I will stretch out My arm and redeem My children from among the nations." As it is written: "For My own sake I will do it, for how can My name be defiled?"

Then the Holy One will reveal His mighty arm to the nations. It will stretch across the whole world, shining with the brilliance of the summer sun at its peak.

In that moment, Israel will be saved from the nations. The Messiah will appear and lead them to Jerusalem with great joy. They will feast and celebrate, glorifying the Messianic Kingdom and the house of David throughout the world. No nation will have power over them anymore. The people of Israel will gather from the four corners of the earth and dine with the Messiah. But the nations of the world will not share in their feast, as it is written:

"The Lord has bared His holy arm in the sight of all the nations, and all the ends of the earth shall see the salvation of our God."

And again: "The Lord alone led him, and there was no foreign god with him."

"And the Lord shall be King over all the earth."

Chapter XLVII (B)

The Divine Flames that go forth from the Throne of Glory, crowned and escorted by numerous angelic hosts through the heavens and back again to the Throne—the angels sing the Holy and the Blessed

Metatron said to me:

These are the seventy-two sacred names that are written upon the heart of the Holy One. They are names of power, righteousness, and majesty: SeDeQ, SaHPeL, SUR, SaDdiQ, SeBa'oTh (Lord of Hosts), ShaDdaY (God Almighty), 'eLoHIM (God), YHWH, and many others of great holiness. Among them are names like ROKeB 'aRaBOTh (He who rides upon the Araboth), HaY (The Living One), and QQQ (Holy, Holy, Holy). Each of these names carries deep meaning and mystery, declaring His eternal glory and dominion. They affirm His strength and wisdom, as written:

"He gives power to the weary and increases strength to those who have no might."

These names are surrounded by countless crowns—crowns of fire, crowns of flame, crowns of chashmal, and crowns of lightning. They are accompanied by thousands upon thousands of powerful angels, carrying them with honor like subjects escorting a mighty king. These angelic hosts surround them with pillars of fire, glowing clouds, flashes of lightning, and brilliant light. Wherever they move, there is awe, trembling, majesty, and deep reverence, along with dignity, glory, wisdom, and understanding. Their journey is marked by the brightness of chashmal and the splendor of divine radiance.

As they travel through the heavens, these sacred names are praised. The angels call out before them, "Holy, Holy, Holy!" The heavenly hosts roll them through the realms of the skies, treating them as honored and mighty princes.

When these names are finally brought back to the Throne of Glory, the Chayyoth surrounding the Merkaba open their mouths in praise. They declare the holiness and greatness of His name, saying:

"Blessed be the Name of His glorious kingdom forever and ever."

Chapter XLVII (C)

An EnochMetatron piece

I took him, strengthened him, and gave him a special purpose. I chose Enoch, my servant, who is unlike any other among the children of heaven. I made him strong during the time of the first Adam. But when I saw how corrupt the people of the flood generation had become, I removed my Shekina from among them. I lifted it up to the heavens with the sound of a trumpet and a mighty shout, as it is written:

"God has gone up with a shout, the Lord with the sound of a trumpet."

I took Enoch, the son of Jared, from among humans and raised him up to the high heavens with the sound of a trumpet and a loud cry. I made him my witness among the Chayyoth of the Merkaba in the world to come. I gave him a throne that stands near my own Throne of Glory, measuring seventy thousand parasangs, all made of fire. I assigned him seventy angels, representing the seventy nations of the world, and gave him authority over all realms, both in heaven and on earth.

I granted him wisdom and understanding greater than all other angels. I gave him the name The Lesser Yah, a name whose Gematria value is seventy-one. I placed him in charge of the works of creation, making his power greater than that of the ministering angels.

I appointed him over all the treasuries and storage places in every heaven and gave him the keys to each one. He became the prince over all heavenly rulers, a minister of the Throne of Glory, and the overseer of the Halls of Araboth, with the authority to open their doors before me. He was given the responsibility to arrange and exalt the Throne of Glory.

I placed him over the Holy Chayyoth, crowning them with honor, and over the majestic Ophannim, strengthening them with glory. He was assigned to clothe the exalted Kerubim with majesty and make the radiant sparks shine with brilliance.

I gave him authority over the flaming Seraphim, covering them with greatness, and over the Chashmallim, filling them with radiant light. His task was to prepare my seat every morning. As the highest prince, he ensured that the Holy Chayyoth were crowned with majesty and clothed with honor, ready to carry out their divine roles.

I seated him before my Throne of Glory so that he could magnify my name in its fullness. He was entrusted with revealing my power and holding the secrets of both the heavens and the earth. He was chosen to witness my greatness as I sat upon my throne in majesty and splendor.

I made him greater than all others, raising him to a height of seventy thousand parasangs among the mighty. His throne was exalted to reflect my own, and its glory was increased to match the honor of my presence.

I transformed his body—his flesh became blazing fire, and his bones turned into burning coals. His eyes shone like flashes of lightning, and his eyebrows glowed with endless light. His face radiated like the sun, and his eyes reflected the majesty of the Throne of Glory.

I dressed him in honor and majesty, wrapping him in beauty and greatness. On his head, I placed a royal crown—a diadem of unmatched brilliance, measuring five hundred by five hundred parasangs. I adorned him with my own honor, majesty, and the splendor that shines from my Throne of Glory.

I called him The Lesser YHWH, The Prince of the Presence, and The Knower of Secrets. I revealed every mystery to him, just as a father shares knowledge with his son. I entrusted him with all secrets, ensuring that he would proclaim them in righteousness and truth.

I established his throne at the entrance to my Hall, where he sits to judge the heavenly hosts. Every prince of heaven stands before him, receiving instructions from him to carry out the will of the Most High.

Seventy names, taken from my own names, were given to him to elevate his status. I placed seventy princes under his command, ensuring they followed my words in every language.

I gave him the power to humble the proud and raise up the lowly. With a single word, he could bring down kings and redirect their paths. He was granted the authority to establish rulers in their positions, as it is written:

"He changes the times and the seasons; He removes kings and sets up kings." (Daniel 2:21)

He was tasked with giving wisdom to the wise and knowledge to those who seek understanding, as it is written:

"And He gives knowledge to those who understand." (Daniel 2:21)

He was chosen to reveal the secrets of my words and teach the laws of my righteous judgment, as it is written:

"So shall my word be that goes forth from my mouth; it shall not return to me empty but shall accomplish what I desire." (Isaiah 55:11)

The phrase "I shall accomplish" is not used, but rather "he shall accomplish", meaning that whatever command comes from the Holy One, Metatron carries it out faithfully. He upholds and establishes the decrees of the Holy One.

I entrusted him with teaching the Law, the Books of Wisdom, the Haggada, and the Tradition, ensuring that those who study them gain complete understanding. As it is written:

"Whom will He teach knowledge? And whom will He make understand tradition? Those weaned from milk, taken from the breast." (Isaiah 28:9)

Chapter XLVII (D)

Metatron has seventy names, which the Holy One took from His own name and gave to him to increase his glory. These names include Yehoel Yah, Yehoel, Yophiel, Aphphiel, Margziel, Simkam, Yahseyah, Ssbibyah, Periel, Tatriel, Tabkiel, and many others. Each name reflects the divine power and holiness given to him. One of these names is The Lesser YHWH, because God's own name is within him, as it is written:

"For My name is in him." (Exodus 23:21)

Another name, Sagnesakiel, refers to his role as the guardian of all the treasuries of wisdom.

All the knowledge of wisdom was entrusted to Metatron, and it was through him that this wisdom was revealed to Moses on Mount Sinai. During the forty days Moses stayed on the mountain, he learned the Torah in seventy forms and seventy languages. He also studied the Prophets, Writings, Halakhas (laws), Traditions, Haggadas, and Toseftas, all in seventy forms and languages. This covered every aspect of divine knowledge and law. However, at the end of the forty days, Moses forgot everything he had learned in an instant.

Then the Holy One called Yephiphyah, the Prince of the Law, and through him, all the knowledge was restored to Moses as a gift. As it is written:

"And the Lord gave them unto me." (Deuteronomy 10:4)

From that moment on, the knowledge remained with Moses forever. And how do we know this? It is written:

"Remember the Law of Moses, My servant, which I commanded him at Horeb for all Israel—My statutes and judgments." (Malachi 4:4)

Here, "the Law of Moses" refers to the Torah, Prophets, and Writings. "Statutes" refer to the Halakhas and Traditions, and "Judgments" refer to the Haggadas and Toseftas. All of this sacred knowledge and wisdom was given to Moses directly from the heavens on Mount Sinai.

The seventy names given to Metatron reflect the Explicit Names engraved on the Merkaba and the Throne of Glory. These sacred names were taken from God's own names and placed upon Metatron. The ministering angels use these seventy names to address the King of Kings in the highest heavens. Alongside these names, there are also twenty-two letters engraved on the ring of His finger. This ring is used to seal the destinies of the heavenly rulers, the Angel of Death, and the fate of every nation on earth.

Metatron is known as the Angel, the Prince of the Presence, and the Prince of Wisdom, Understanding, Kings, Rulers, and Glory. He was honored above all the great beings of heaven and earth. He himself testified, saying:

"The God of Israel is my witness that when I revealed this great secret to Moses, all the heavenly hosts rose up against me in outrage."

The angels demanded to know why such sacred knowledge—the very secret by which the heavens, the earth, the seas, the mountains, the rivers, Gehenna, the Garden of Eden, the Tree of Life, and even the Torah itself were created—was given to a mortal man.

"Why would you share this with someone born of a woman, a being made of flesh, imperfect and unclean? Did you get permission from the heavens? Were you granted authority from the Holy Place?"

In response, Metatron declared that the Holy One had indeed given him the authority and permission to reveal these secrets. But the angels were still not satisfied until God Himself stepped in. He rebuked them and said:

"I delight in Metatron, my servant. I have chosen him, loved him, and entrusted him with these mysteries. He is unique among all the children of heaven."

With God's approval, Metatron took these treasures of wisdom and revealed them to Moses. Moses then passed them on to Joshua, who gave them to the elders. The elders then passed them down to the prophets, and from the prophets, they were entrusted to the men of the Great Synagogue.

From there, they were handed to Ezra the Scribe, then to Hillel the Elder, and later to R. Abbahu, who passed them to R. Zera. R. Zera then entrusted them to the men of faith, whose role was to use this knowledge to guide, warn, and heal all the diseases afflicting the world.

As it is written:

"If you listen carefully to the voice of the Lord your God, do what is right in His eyes, pay attention to His commands, and keep all His laws, I will not bring upon you any of the diseases I brought upon Egypt, for I am the Lord who heals you." (Exodus 15:26)

And so, this sacred wisdom was passed down through the generations, preserving the knowledge and healing power entrusted by the Creator of the World.

(Ended and finished. Praise be to the Creator of the World.)

Thank You for Reading

Dear Reader,

We hope this timeless classic has sparked your imagination and enriched your literary journey. Now that you've turned the final page, we want to share a vision for the future of reading—one where every classic you've ever wanted to explore is at your fingertips, in a format that best suits your life.

We'd like to invite you to gain immediate, unlimited digital & audiobook access to hundreds of the most treasured literary classics ever written—along with the option to secure deluxe paperback, hardcover & box set editions at printing cost. Together, we can spark a new global literary renaissance alongside our small, independent publishing house called "The Library of Alexandria."

Thousands of years ago, the Library of Alexandria stood as a beacon of knowledge—until it was lost to history. We aim to reignite that spirit of preservation and discovery right now, in the modern age—only this time, it's accessible to all, in every language and every format.

Picture a world where every timeless classic, novel, poem, or philosophical treatise is not only available to read but also updated for today's readers—modernized, translated into any language or dialect, and ready to enjoy in any format you choose, whether that is in an eBook, audiobook, paperback, or deluxe hardcover & box set version a printing cost.

By joining our movement to rebuild the modern Library of Alexandria, you become part of an unprecedented mission to offer:

- **Unlimited Audiobook & eBook Access to the Greatest Classics of All Time**

Instantly explore thousands of legendary works, from Plato and Shakespeare to Jane Austen and Leo Tolstoy. All are instantly ready to read or listen to, giving you a complete literary universe at your fingertips.

- **Paperback & Deluxe Editions at Printing Costs:**

Purchase any title in a paperback, deluxe hardbound, or deluxe boxset edition at printing costs, shipped right to your doorstep. Curate your personal library of Alexandria with editions worthy of display—crafted to last, designed to captivate, and delivered straight to your door.

- **Modern translations for Contemporary Readers in all languages and dialects**

Discover a vast selection of classics reimagined in clear, current language—no more struggling with outdated phrases or obscure references. Next to the original versions, we aim to offer translations in as many languages and dialects as possible.

As we continue our translation efforts and add new languages, readers everywhere can connect with these works as if they were written today. By bridging linguistic divides, you're contributing to ensuring that these timeless stories become more meaningful, accessible, and inspiring for people across the globe.

- **Your Personal Library of Alexandria:**

Over the months and years, you'll curate a unique physical archive of classics—each volume a testament to your taste, curiosity, and love of knowledge. It's not just about owning books—it's about curating a cultural legacy you'll cherish and pass down for generations to come.

- **Join a Global Literary Renaissance:**

Your support fuels an ongoing mission: allowing us to reinvest in offering deluxe print editions (including special boxsets) at their true cost, broaden the range of available formats and translations, and extend the reach of these works to new audiences worldwide. By joining today, you're not just preserving a legacy of masterpieces; you set in motion a powerful wave of literary accessibility.

We are more than a publisher—we're a movement, and we can't do it alone. Your support lets us scale our mission, preserving and reimagining history's greatest works for tomorrow's readers.

Become a Torchbearer of knowledge.

Thank you for picking up this book and allowing us into your literary journey. As you turn the pages, know that you're part of something larger: a global effort to keep these stories alive, share their wisdom across borders and generations, and spark a true cultural revival for the modern era.

If this resonates with you—please consider taking the next step by visiting:

www.libraryofalexandria.com

With gratitude and a shared love of knowledge,

The Modern Library of Alexandria Team

Visit:

www.libraryofalexandria.com

Or scan the code below:

www.ingramcontent.com/pod-product-compliance
Lightning Source LLC
Chambersburg PA
CBHW011204090426
42742CB00019B/3400